knitted

FINGER PUPPETS

34 Easy-to-Make Toys

Meg Leach

Martingale®
& COMPANY

Knitted Finger Puppets: 34 Easy-to-Make Toys
© 2008 by Meg Leach

Martingale®
& COMPANY

Martingale & Company®
20205 144th Ave. NE
Woodinville, WA 98072-8478 USA
www.martingale-pub.com

Printed in China
13 12 11 10 09 08   8 7 6 5 4 3 2 1

Library of Congress Cataloging-in-Publication Data
Library of Congress Control Number: 2008031664

ISBN: 978-1-56477-887-1

MISSION STATEMENT

Dedicated to providing quality products and service to inspire creativity.

CREDITS

President & CEO: Tom Wierzbicki

Publisher: Jane Hamada

Editorial Director: Mary V. Green

Managing Editor: Tina Cook

Technical Editor: Donna Druchunas

Copy Editor: Sheila Chapman Ryan

Design Director: Stan Green

Production Manager: Regina Girard

Illustrator: Robin Strobel

Cover & Text Designer: Regina Girard

Photographer: Brent Kane

Dedication

*To David, Christi, Will, and Max,
my very excellent and imaginative
technical advisors, who know just
how wizards and dragons and tigers
should look.*

CONTENTS

Christmas at the North Pole

Under the Big Top

The Enchanted Forest

The Enchanted Forest

the joys of FINGER

There are many reasons to love making finger puppets. They are relatively quick to make. The directions are easy and require only a basic knowledge of knitting and crochet. Making them is a great way to use up all those little balls of yarn left over from years of knitting hats and sweaters. It's certainly a very creative endeavor. But most of all I make puppets because they are so personal. Knitting a mother monkey and her baby for a niece or a ballerina puppet for a 5-year-old ballerina brings me special joy. Some of the first puppets I made 40 years ago for a very special little girl are now lovingly stored in her sewing basket, not to be played with anymore, but treasured for the memories.

The very first puppet I knit in 1968 was a baby monkey made with brown fingering yarn and size 1 (2.25 mm) double-pointed needles. The tiny head had only nine stitches and nine rounds. The body had 10 stitches and 11 rounds. I crocheted little arms, feet, and a tail, and added a small face of felt stuffed with yarn. I lost the original but I've made many since then and have improved on that first one by increasing and decreasing stitches for more shaping and changing colors to match beloved cartoon characters.

I was introduced to this delightful hobby by my friend Susan Hunt, who had discovered the finger-puppet patterns for the Three Little Pigs and the Wolf in a 1968 *Crafts* magazine. Those original instructions called for fingering-weight yarn. But shortly after making a few sets of these, a knitter in my hometown gave me a box of her leftover worsted-weight yarn, and I discovered that while it's sometimes harder to work with the thicker yarn and maybe a little less elegant, the product is more durable for children's play and also more likely to fit adult fingers.

PUPPETS

Over the years I've made more than 250 of these 3" to 4" creations for family and friends. Since 1971 I've made finger puppets for each holiday or special event for my son, including a football player, a bride and groom, a bearded fisherman, and two babies—one with blue eyes and one with brown. Those two babies, my grandsons Will and Max, have been the motivation for a flurry of puppet-making activity in the last six years.

church services thanks to a purse full of finger puppets. In this era of computer games and cell phones, finger puppets offer the antidote to noisy gadgets—no batteries required.

While you may be thinking about the children in your life as you look through this book, some of the most enthusiastic responses have come from adults. A tiny kitten puppet for a friend who loves cats or a white-haired queen for a friend turning 60 were definitely worth the effort. You'll never run out of characters to try or reasons to make them.

If all the aforementioned reasons for knitting finger puppets aren't enough, consider that finger puppets pack very easily into backpacks, purses, and diaper bags and provide hours of quiet play in places where that's essential, such as airplanes, doctors' offices, churches, and long car rides. One family of very active little boys enjoyed years of peaceful weekly

Warning: Choking Hazard

Puppets with small parts that are glued or sewn on are not suitable for children under three years old. Use embroidery to embellish toys for young children. Make sure you always supervise children when they play with the puppets.

USING THIS BOOK

The first part of this book is all about the special techniques needed to make puppets. Most require only basic knitting skills, but there are some special skills that you will find helpful.

The wonderful inhabitants of the North Pole can be found in the second section. There are eight patterns in this collection: Santa, Mrs. Claus, an elf, a snowman, a penguin, and, of course, a reindeer. There are even patterns for the toy car and the teddy bear that Santa will be giving away on Christmas Eve.

The most challenging section is "Under the Big Top," which includes circus characters. The I-cord method for creating the elephants' trunks and the trapeze lady's legs is a recent discovery for me. The long necks of the giraffes and their expanded bodies also posed some challenges. I must have experimented on a dozen of them before I found a fairly simple approach that matched the image in my head, and the door to a whole new list of characters was open to me.

You will also find a section of patterns for characters who live in "The Enchanted Forest." Hansel and Gretel, a witch, the Three Little Pigs, and the Big Bad Wolf are just some of the characters who will come alive on your fingers when you tell the favorite stories.

The real fun begins in the final section, when you can start to create your own characters. When you begin to make a finger puppet, start by considering the most-likely shape of the head. Is the character's head long and narrow, round, pear-shaped, pointed, flat-topped, or maybe even elliptical (as many cartoon characters' seem to be)? What color do you want it to be?

Then consider the body. While body shapes are somewhat limited because you need to accommodate small fingers, there are several body options suggested in this section. You might choose the basic shape, or the muscleman, princess, or wizard. And for any

character you create you get to decide on what colors to use, which is only difficult because there are so many choices!

The colors, size, and shape can all be varied enough to bring sufficient realism to any puppet. To add even more personality to each character, you can choose the hair color and style and the eye color and size. Mouths, ears, and noses can be varied, and you can add glasses, a crown, or a hat to complete the special persona.

So, pick up a set of size 1 (2.25 mm) double-pointed needles, a size D-3 (3.25 mm) crochet hook, and a variety pack of sewing needles. Find a comfortable chair, and then reach into your basket of leftover yarns. Choose a color and shape for the head and body. Stitch on a special hairdo, add some eyes, a nose, and two ears. Maybe add a bit of lace around the neck or a piece of brown felt to make a vest. That tiny hat you found at the craft store would be perfect. Surely that jar of sequins can be used somewhere. See how it goes? See the smile on that child's face? It is a most wonderful passion. Enjoy.

KNITTING BASICS

Unlike fitted knitting projects, precise instructions are not essential here. One more round or stitch won't ruin the look. Two more rounds may change the proportion a little but call that your creative license. Maybe your wolf needs to be really, really big and menacing—so add another stitch or another round. And don't worry about gauge because medium-weight yarn comes in several thicknesses, and the differences are not significant. Look at the three wolves shown here. The wolf on the left, I made with gray yarn of unknown origin found at the bottom of my knitting basket. The very beautiful gray wolf created from Encore yarn and the wolf made with

Camouflage by Bernat follow the same pattern but are just a little different in size.

Creating these little puppets doesn't take advanced skills. If you know how to cast on, increase, and decrease, you're well on your way to a puppet menagerie.

Skill Levels

◼◻◻◻ **Beginner:** *Projects for first-time knitters using basic knit and purl stitches. Minimal shaping.*

◼◼◻◻ **Easy:** *Projects using basic stitches, repetitive stitch patterns, and simple color changes. Simple shaping.*

◼◼◼◻ **Intermediate:** *Projects using a variety of stitches, such as basic cables and lace, simple intarsia, and techniques for double-pointed needles and knitting in the round. Midlevel shaping and finishing.*

◼◼◼◼ **Experienced:** *Projects using advanced techniques and stitches, such as short rows, Fair Isle, more intricate intarsia, cables, lace patterns, and numerous color changes.*

All puppets are knit in the round. Although this is often considered an intermediate skill,

once you get the feel and routine of knitting on double-pointed needles, you won't have any trouble with the patterns. I've marked most of the puppets as easy because I believe you can make them with just a little practice.

Cinderella, her prince, and most of the animal faces use increases and decreases for shaping. Sometimes those stitches can take time because you are using such small needles on worsted-weight yarn.

The giraffe, reindeer, and the elephant require the most experience due to the the curves of their heads and the cording for the elephant's trunk.

One of the easiest personalities is Hansel (page 44). He has a basic round head, a basic body shape, and straight stitches for his hair. Start there if you are a beginner and you'll get hooked.

9

I learned to knit when I was in grade school. But like many long-time knitters I learned from someone—not from a book or set of instructions. It was years before I realized that I wasn't casting on in any method that was considered "correct." I just looped the yarn around the needle in some fashion and started knitting. When I finally discovered that there was a "right" way to cast on, I also discovered that there were many "right" ways to cast on. I use the same techniques I've been using for about 25 years, and they've worked well for these little characters. In the following sections, I provide instructions for some special techniques that you'll need to know especially for knitting finger puppets.

DOUBLE-POINTED NEEDLES (DPNS)

Knitting on double-pointed needles, especially size 1 (2.25 mm) and especially with worsted-weight yarn, can take some practice. But remember that most of these puppets have fewer than 24 stitches and 24 rounds.

Cast on the number of stitches required in the pattern. Starting with the last stitch you cast on, distribute the stitches as evenly as possible onto three double-pointed needles. Be careful not to twist the stitches (make sure that you can see the purl side of the stitches on the inside of the needles). All the little bumps on the back of the cast-on row should be evenly spaced.

Hold the three needles together in a triangle with the yarn in your left hand. Now pick up the fourth needle and knit the first stitch on the left needle. You'll need to be sure to tighten this first stitch to prevent a gap in your work. This is called joining. Continue to work all the stitches on all three needles. You may want to put a tiny knitting marker at the place where you started the first round. That gives you a reminder for counting the number of rounds. The best place for a marker is between the first and second stitch so it doesn't fall off easily. Or you can tie a piece of

yarn around the first needle. The yarn seems to stay in place better. Each time you knit all the stitches on all three needles, that is called a round (rnd).

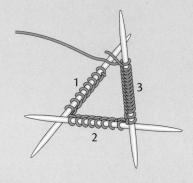

DECREASING AND INCREASING

This is what gives the puppets their unique faces and shapes. Four decreases on round 10, and then four increases on round 14, give Cinderella (page 46) the perfect ball gown. A couple of decreases at the back of Giraffe (page 37) gives him just the right shape on which to hang his tail! There is a trick to increases and decreases when the project is so small. For one thing the stitches need to be as invisible as possible, and they need to slant in the right direction. With such small pieces, try to knit the stitches a little bit loosely so that the increases and decreases are easier to complete.

Slanting increases and decreases in mirror images creates symmetrical shapes.

Decreasing

Left slant: slip, slip, knit (ssk): Slip one stitch from the left needle to the right needle as if to knit. Slip the next stitch from the left needle to the right needles as if to knit. They have to be done separately. Then insert the left needle into these two stitches from left to right and knit them together.

Right slant (K2tog): Insert the right-hand needle into the next two stitches on the left-hand needle, from left to right. Knit them together as one stitch.

Increasing

Increases may cause some frustration at first because you are working with such small needles, but it is worth the difficulty because the shaping is so necessary and the result will be wonderful.

Left-slant increase (M1L): With the left needle, pick up the strand between the last stitch knit on the right needle and the next stitch to be knit on the left needle from the front. With the right needle, knit into the back of that loop.

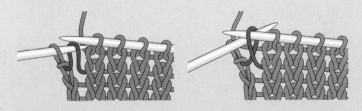

Right-slant increase (M1R): With the left needle, pick up the strand between the last stitch knit on the right needle and the next stitch to be knit on the left needle from the back. With the right needle, knit into the front of the left needle.

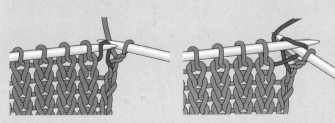

FINISHING HEADS AND BODIES

When you have come to the top of the head or the body, there are several ways to end. One way is to slip all the stitches off the needles onto the yarn tail using a tapestry needle and pull them tight. That gives the top of the head or shoulders a nice rounded appearance. Another method is to weave the stitches together using the Kitchener stitch. Weaving gives a more defined shoulder appearance that is perfect for the prince or muscleman puppets. It also gives tigers, wolves, and other animals the right shape and a place to put their ears.

Yarn Overs

I was excited when I discovered that sock heel instructions were the best for making the heads of some animal characters—elephants, giraffes, and reindeer. The directions are easy enough, especially with a simplified method for "turning the heel." Partway through the row, when it's time to start the shaping, turn the work to go back the other way and make a yarn over. When the shaping is finished, knit the yarn overs together with the next stitch. It's as simple as that!

As careful as I was in the beginning, I wasn't satisfied with the purl yarn overs. There were holes in the left side of every animal. The wonderful knitters at the 3 Kittens Needle Art Shop in Lilydale, Minnesota, took time to help me. Looping the yarn over the needle as shown in the art below makes a lovely "hole-less" face.

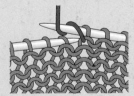
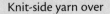

Knit-side yarn over   Purl-side yarn over

Gathering and Tying Off

Cut the yarn, leaving a tail about 10" long (or the length specified in the pattern.). Thread the tail into a tapestry needle. Insert the needle into all the stitches remaining on the double-pointed needles, remove the knitting needles, and pull the yarn tight so there are no holes at the top. Make a small knot and pull the yarn back inside the head or body. When you pull the yarn inside the head you will then use that yarn to make the ears and nose, so be sure you have enough yarn remaining. Instructions for making ears and noses are on page 61.

Gather off the bottom of the heads after you have made the ears and/or nose and stuffed the head with leftover yarn or other filler. Pick up the end of the yarn from casting on and thread it into a tapestry needle. Then insert the needle into every one of the cast-on stitches, pull tight, and knot it. Leave the end for attaching to the body.

Kitchener Stitch

The woven top is called the Kitchener stitch. It makes such an elegant weave that it is worth mastering.

The front and back of the prince's shoulders and the top of the pig's head are joined with the Kitchener stitch.

Needle 1: Knit and slip, purl and leave. Needle 2: purl and slip, knit and leave. This is my shorthand to remember the pattern: KPPK.

Now here is how it works: cut the yarn, leaving a 24" tail. Thread the yarn onto a tapestry needle. Put all the stitches in the knit piece on two knitting needles, with the stitches from the front of the body on one needle and the stitches from the back of the body on the other. Hold the knitting needles parallel. You need an equal number of stitches on each needle. (If you end up with an extra stitch, do another round and decrease one stitch first.) Then, with the two needles together, begin by using the tapestry needle to take the first stitch off the front needle as if to knit. Pull the yarn through and pull it tight. Insert the tapestry needle into the next stitch on the front needle as if to purl but *leave it on the knitting needle* and pull the thread through. Now go to the back needle and thread the needle through the first stitch as if to purl and take it off the knitting needle. Run the yarn through this stitch and pull it tight. Insert the tapestry needle into the next stitch on the back needle as if to knit. Leave that stitch on the back needle. Now return to the stitch that was left on the front needle and insert the tapestry needle as if to knit and slip it off, pulling the yarn tight. Continue in this manner until all stitches are removed.

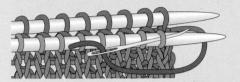

Take first stitch off needle as if to knit.

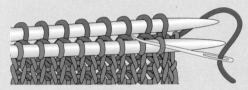

Insert in next stitch as if to purl.
Leave stitch on needle.

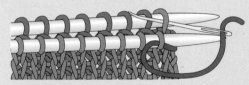

Take first stitch off back needle as if to purl.

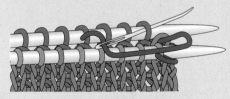

Insert in next stitch as if to knit.
Leave stitch on needle.

Take stitch off front needle as if to knit.

I-Cord

I-cord makes great legs for the trapeze lady and the ballerina. With two double-pointed needles, cast on three stitches. Knit three and do not turn. Slide the stitches to the beginning of the needle and knit three. Repeat this pattern until the leg is long enough for your character, usually 8 to 10 rounds. You may also use the I-cord for arms.

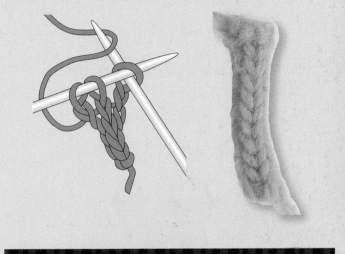

Weaving in Ends

When you cast on, make sure to leave a 12" tail. When you have finished the puppet, weave this end through the cast-on stitches and cut it off. Use the end of the cast-on stitches on the head to stitch back and forth through the body for stability. The same technique should be used on the tying-off yarn for the body. Leave enough yarn to stitch into the head and back again. Then cut it off. Sometimes I leave enough to make arms but it is just as easy to cut a new piece for those. When you are tying off the top of the head, leave enough yarn to make the ears and nose and then leave the end inside the head with the other stuffing. Any other yarn or threads from the embroidery work can be threaded back and forth through the head and then cut off.

CROCHET BASICS

I use crochet for the arms on most of my puppets. The Big Bad Wolf (page 54) needed thick, short arms so I used a double strand of yarn and made only five chains. Mother Monkey (page 34) needed very long, slender arms and legs so I used a single strand of yarn and 10 chains. (If you don't crochet, you can use a three-stitch I-cord for the arms instead.)

CHAIN

From the inside of the puppet, insert a tapestry needle with about 36" of yarn. Take a stitch to make the first loop, which you then transfer to a crochet hook (the hook size will be stated in the pattern). Wrap the yarn around the hook counterclockwise and draw it back through the loop. Repeat until you have the required number of stitches. Then turn and begin to slip-stitch your way back to the first stitch.

SLIP STITCH

Insert the hook in the top of the second chain from the hook, yarn over the hook in a counterclockwise direction, and draw a loop through the stitch and through the loop on the hook. Repeat until you reach the beginning stitch. Pull the yarn through this last stitch and repeat on the other side of the body for the second arm. I often use a smaller crochet hook for the slip stitch than I did for the chain, either because I need a smaller arm or because it's easier to pick up the stitch with the type of yarn I'm using.

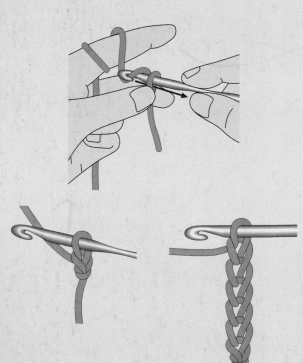

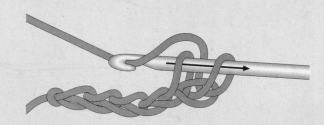

Supplies

Finger puppets are made with the same supplies as most other knitting projects, except that they are made with double-pointed needles, and some special notions are used for embellishments.

YARNS

Finger puppets are made for play. The fingering-weight yarn I used for the very first puppets may have produced an elegant product, but it wasn't rugged and didn't stand the test of time. I learned a lot about yarns as I began to experiment with the leftover yarns I had in boxes and baskets around my house. Sometimes two yellow giraffes made with the same number of stitches and rounds wouldn't be the same finished size because one yarn was wool and one was acrylic. For me it's more about the color than the fiber content of the yarn or the exact size.

There are many small balls of yarn in my baskets that have long since lost any identification, so I usually do a sample to test how well the yarn will knit and what size it's likely to be. You can determine quickly if the yarn you are testing will work for the puppet you envisioned by knitting a small sample of six or seven stitches for five or six rounds.

I choose yarn that will be easy to increase and decrease and will also hold its shape so it can sit on a shelf; the puppet also needs to fit as well on an adult's finger as on a child's. And, of course, it has to be just the right color. Listed below are a few brand names of yarn that I like to use.

One of my favorites is Plymouth's Encore, which is a blend of 75% acrylic and 25% wool. It comes in beautiful colors and is easy to work with. The puppets made with it aren't quite able to stand up by themselves, so I sometimes purl the first row when I use this yarn. Reynold's Utopia or Caron's worsted-weight yarns are 100% acrylic and just a little harder to use if you're doing a lot of decreases or increases, but they will last through many playtimes. I love Patons's 100% wool. The softness lends itself to some of the sweetest characters and it should last for many years. Red Heart's Soft Yarn is 100% acrylic and has a warm, lovely sheen that is perfect for robes and gowns.

For a very long time I searched for the right skin tones. Some of the browns were very good but the pinks were too pink. So I dyed light pink worsted yarn in tea. Sometimes I left it in the tea for a short time and sometimes I left it for a very long time. Then the owner of Zandy's Yarn Etc. in Burnsville, Minnesota, suggested Paternayan Persian yarns. The yarns are so lovely and there is a lot of color variety to reflect different skin tones. I buy them in small amounts in the embroidery section and I buy some colors in bulk online. It was a wonderful discovery. They make a slightly smaller head than a regular worsted-weight yarn—but then real heads are usually smaller than real bodies.

To stuff the puppets, you can buy fiberfill or another material, but I just use leftover yarn because I always have so much of it on hand. It also lends itself well to shaping.

NEEDLES, NEEDLES, AND NEEDLES

First you'll need to find size 1 (2.25 mm) double-pointed needles that are 7" long. (Some knitters may prefer the shorter 4"-long glove needles.) I have them in plastic, wood, and metal. They'll all work well and are interchangeable so if you lose a metal one you can substitute with a needle out of the plastic group.

I always have a large selection of tapestry needles stuck in a pin cushion ready to be used for attaching heads to bodies, stitching on hair, or starting the chaining on the arms. It's important to have a good supply of embroidery needles for the eyes, mouth, and any clothing designs you may want to add. I also have a supply of very small sewing needles for invisible stitching of eyes, beads, or felt.

CROCHET HOOKS

Most of the patterns call for size D-3 (3.25 mm) crochet hook. But I also keep a supply of sizes C-2–G-6 (2.75 mm–4 mm) handy for unusual projects. I prefer the metal hooks because they seem to give a more even stitch and they are better at picking up the small stitches.

ESSENTIALS

In addition to yarn and needles, you'll need the following supplies for the projects in this book.

- Scissors (a small pair for snipping yarn and a pair of craft scissors for cutting felt)
- Safety pins (for holding back stitches)
- Straight pins (for holding pieces together while you sew and for marking places for ears, arms, and noses)
- Stitch markers (choose the smallest size)

You should also have a good selection of embroidery floss on hand. My mother loved to do cross-stitch and I have her amazing collection of embroidery floss in many, many colors. Start with the basic package of red, blue, green, yellow, brown, white, and black. Sometimes for larger mouths or eyes I'll use several strands of a color and sometimes I use just one strand to get the right effect. One strand of gold thread is all you need for Grandma's glasses (page 53).

NOTIONS

Knitting these little bodies and heads is fun and can easily be done in a couple of hours. It's the next part that can be so creative and so addictive. It's so hard to walk into a craft shop and not see some tiny trinket, bead, or piece of felt that would be perfect for a little princess, superhero, or teddy bear. When I showed my grandsons Wizard's body (page 41) and asked for suggestions for his hat, they wanted it to be a big black one. At the craft store I found black felt with sparkles on it, and in the next row there were metal stars for embellishment, and then I discovered the gold pipe cleaner for his wand and a wooden bead for his pot of magic potion! Then there are the laces that come in every width, thickness, and color. Gold laces make spectacular crowns or trim for royal robes. Though they may seem expensive, it takes only 3" to 4" to make a crown.

I like using felt for ears, snouts, tummies, and hats because it can be stitched on invisibly. With a very small needle, slide a single thread between the back of the felt and the top of the knit piece. Below are some suggestions for additional embellishments:

- Beads come in many colors and sizes and can be used for eyes or jewelry
- Sequins are great for belt buckles and sometimes for scary eyes
- Miniatures of everything—hats, toys, drums, tools
- Buttons
- Scrapbook art and notions (the elf's hammer on page 22 is a paper scrapbook embellishment)
- Embroidery floss, including silver and gold thread
- Pipe cleaners
- Small flowers and baskets
- Ribbons

Abbreviations

approx	approximately
beg	begin(ning)
BO	bind off
CC	contrasting color
ch	chain
cont	continue(ing)
dec	decrease(ing)
dpn(s)	double-pointed needle(s)
foll	follow(s)(ing)
inc	increase(ing)
K	knit
K2tog	knit 2 stitches together—1 stitch decreased (page 11)
kw	knitwise
M1L	make 1 stitch with a left slant (page 11)
M1R	make 1 stitch with a right slant (page 11)
MC	main color
P	purl
P2tog	purl 2 stitches together—1 stitch decreased
pw	purlwise
rep(s)	repeat(s)
rnd(s)	round(s)
sl	slip
sl st	stitch—slip stitches purlwise unless instructed otherwise
ssk	slip 2 stitches knitwise, 1 at a time, to right needle, then insert left needle from left to right into front loops and knit 2 stitches together—1 stitch decreased (page 11)
st(s)	stitch(es)
tbl	through back loop(s)
tog	together
WS	wrong side
YO(s)	yarn over(s) (page 11)

CHRISTMAS AT THE NORTH POLE

This collection of Christmas puppets makes a delightful pre-Christmas gift for the little ones in your life. They will have such fun setting up Santa's workshop with Mrs. Claus, the elf, a reindeer, and the snowman all there to help. And the teddy bear and toy car are all ready to be placed in someone's stocking for Christmas morning.

Skill Levels: Reindeer's head and neck require increases, decreases, and yarn overs, which classify him as **Experienced.** ■■■■

All the others are **Easy.** ■■□□

Santa Claus

SUPPLIES

Red, white, brown, and pink (or color of choice for skin) worsted-weight yarn **4**

Size 1 (2.25 mm) double-pointed needles

Size D-3 (3.25 mm) crochet hook

Embroidery floss for glasses, mouth, and eyes in the colors of your choice

Tapestry, embroidery, and sewing needles

Invisible or pink sewing thread

Yarn scraps or fiberfill for stuffing

Craft glue

Other: small piece of black felt, gold sequin, miniature toy, and small bell (optional)

BODY

With red yarn, CO 22 sts. Place sts onto 3 dpns and join.

Rnds 1–18: Knit.

Rnd 19: (K2, ssk, K3, K2tog, K2) twice.

Gather and tie off at top, leaving 6" for attaching to head.

Arms: Attach 36" of red yarn at one side of body. Make st and then, using crochet hook, ch 10 sts, turn and sl st into second ch from hook and next 8 sts. Pull yarn through and rep on other side. With tapestry needle and white yarn, sew small yarn loops at cuffs and run strand of white yarn around bottom in running st for trim.

Belt: Cut a ¼"-wide strip of black felt. Tack it in place with needle and sewing thread, and then tack on a gold sequin for buckle.

HEAD

With pink yarn, CO 13 sts. Place sts onto 3 dpns and join.

Rnds 1–11: Knit.

Gather and tie off at top, leaving 12" for nose and ears. Stuff lightly. Gather at bottom and leave 6" for attaching to body.

Attach head to body: Pull the yarn ends back and forth through head and body and then, using sewing needle and thread, attach head to body with small sts.

HAIR

Santa has curly white hair and a beard. For these curls, use tapestry needle and white yarn to make small, loose sts on the face and around head. Make a few sts under the nose for a moustache. Don't pull the sts tight. The hat will cover the top of the head so there is no need to cover that part with white hair too.

HAT

With red yarn, CO 18 sts. Place sts onto 3 dpns and join.

Rnd 1: Purl.

Rnds 2, 4, 6, 8, and 10: Knit.

Rnds 3, 5, 7, and 9: K2tog at beg of each needle—6 sts rem after rnd 9.

Gather and tie off.

Sew a few loops of white yarn or small bell to top of hat.

FACE

With pink yarn and tapestry needle, make a French knot for nose and small knots for ears.

With embroidery needle and floss, embroider glasses, make small French knots for eyes, and embroider a small mouth under mustache.

ACCESSORIES

Bag for toys: With brown yarn, CO 12 sts, leaving a 6" tail to make a handle for Santa to throw over his shoulder. Place sts onto 3 needles and join.

Rnds 1–6: Knit.

Rnd 7: K2, M1R at beg of each needle—15 sts.

Rnds 8–11: Knit.

Gather the 15 sts for bottom of bag. Stuff lightly and glue miniature toy sticking out of top of bag. Put Santa's hands tog and tack bag's handle to his hands.

Mrs. Claus

SUPPLIES

Red, white, and pink (or color of choice for skin) worsted-weight yarn (4)

Size 1 (2.25 mm) double-pointed needles

Size D-3 (3.25 mm) crochet hook

Embroidery floss for glasses, mouth, and eyes in the colors of your choice

Tapestry, embroidery, and sewing needles

Invisible or pink sewing thread

Yarn scraps or fiberfill for stuffing

Other: lace, beads

BODY

Using red yarn, CO 20 sts. Place sts onto 3 dpns and join.

Rnd 1: Purl.

Rnds 2–12: Knit.

Rnd 13: (K1, ssk, K4, K2tog, K1) twice—16 sts.

Rnds 14–20: Knit.

Gather and tie off, leaving 12" for attaching to head.

Arms: Attach 36" of red yarn to one side of body. Make st and then, using crochet hook, ch 10 sts, turn and sl st into second chain and in next 8 sts. Pull yarn through to other side and rep for second arm.

HEAD

With pink yarn, CO 12 sts. Place sts onto 3 dpns and join.

Rnds 1–10: Knit.

Gather and tie off at top, leaving 12" for nose and ears. Stuff lightly. Gather at bottom and leave 6" for attaching to body.

Attach head to body: Pull yarn ends back and forth through head and body and then, using sewing needle and thread, attach head to body with small sts.

Hair: Using tapestry needle and white yarn, give Mrs. Claus white yarn curls by taking small, very loose sts all over her head; or make long sts of white yarn from back and front to top. Then add loose sts for curls at top.

Face: Using embroidery needle and floss, embroider eyes and smile. Using tapestry needle and pink yarn, make a small French knot for nose and small French knots for ears.

ACCESSORY OPTIONS

Tack on a bit of lace for shawl or apron.

Embroider glasses with gold or silver floss.

Sew beads at base of ears for earrings.

Sew on a pearl necklace.

Elf

SUPPLIES

Light green, dark green, and pink (or color of choice for skin) worsted-weight yarn (4)

Pink worsted-weight yarn (4)

Size 1 (2.25 mm) double-pointed needles

Size D-3 (3.25 mm) crochet hook

Embroidery floss for eyes and mouth in the colors of your choice

Tapestry, embroidery, and sewing needles

Invisible or green sewing thread

Yarn scraps or fiberfill for stuffing

Other: jingle bell, paper hammer (a scrapbook embellishment), craft glue

BODY

With dark green yarn, CO 15 sts. Place sts onto 3 dpns and join.

Rnds 1–6: Knit.

Drop dark green, do not cut. Tie on light green.

Rnds 7 and 8: Knit.

Cut light green. Pick up dark green.

Rnds 9–11: Knit.

Gather and tie off at top. Leave 12" for attaching to head.

Arms: Attach 2 strands, 36" long, of dark green at shoulder. Hold strands tog and using crochet hook, ch 7, turn and sl st into second ch from hook and in next 5 chs. Pull yarn through to other side, attach and rep on other side.

Hands (optional): With crochet hook, pull piece of pink yarn through the first ch on arm. Knot it and fray ends for fingers. Rep on other side for other hand.

HEAD AND HAT

Using pink yarn, CO 11 sts. Place sts onto 3 dpns and join.

Rnds 1–6: Knit.

Change to dark green, leaving 6" of pink for nose.

Rnds 7, 8, 10, and 12: Knit.

Rnd 9: K4, ssk, K2tog, K3—9 sts.

Rnd 11: K4, K2tog, K3—8 sts.

Rnd 13: K3, K2tog, K3—7 sts.

Rnd 14: Knit.

Gather and tie off at top. Stuff lightly. Gather at bottom and leave 6" for attaching to body.

Attach head to body: Pull yarn ends back and forth through head and body and then, using sewing needle and thread, attach head to body with small sts.

Face: Using embroidery needle and floss, embroider eyes and mouth in desired colors. Using tapestry needle and pink yarn, make a small French knot for nose.

Ears: Attach 1 strand of pink yarn to side of head. With crochet hook, ch 4 and st to hat. Rep on the other side for second ear.

ACCESSORIES

With sewing needle and thread, tack jingle bell to top of hat. Glue hammer to one hand.

Snowman

Knit a pretty hat to turn this pattern into a snow woman.

SUPPLIES

White and red or green worsted-weight yarn 4

Size 1 (2.25 mm) double-pointed needles

Size D-3 (3.25 mm) crochet hook

Black, red, and orange embroidery floss for eyes, nose, and mouth

Tapestry, embroidery, and sewing needles

Invisible or black sewing thread

Yarn scraps or fiberfill for stuffing

Craft glue (optional)

Other: black felt, small bell (optional)

BODY

Using white yarn, CO 14 sts. Place sts onto 3 dpns and join.

Rnds 1–12: Knit.

Gather and tie off. Leave a 6" tail for attaching body to head.

HEAD

Using white yarn, CO 12 sts. Place sts onto 3 dpns and join.

Rnds 1–10: Knit.

Gather and tie off at top. Stuff lightly and gather at bottom, leaving 6" for attaching to body.

Attach head to body: Pull yarn ends back and forth through head and body and then, using sewing needle and thread, attach head to body with small sts.

FACE

Using embroidery needle and floss, make French knots for eyes with black and st mouth with red thread.

Using crochet hook, attach orange floss at the spot for the nose. Ch 4, turn, sl st in second ch from hook and in next st. Tie off.

ACCESSORIES

Scarf: With crochet hook and green or red yarn, ch 20. Tie off and tie around neck.

Snowman's hat: Cut a small half circle of black felt (pattern below). Wrap and st it into a cone. Stretch the outer edges of the cone to create a brim. With sewing needle and black thread, attach hat to head and push point of cone inside to fashion a flat-top hat shape. St in place.

Snow woman's hat: To make a hat for a snow woman, using red or green yarn, CO 12 sts. Place sts onto 3 dpns and join. Knit 6 rnds. Gather and tie off for a stocking hat. Sew to head and, if desired, tack a bell to the top.

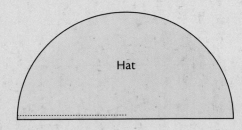

Hat

Reindeer

SUPPLIES

Brown, white, red, and beige (or color of choice for muzzle) worsted-weight yarn (4)

Size 1 (2.5 mm) double-pointed needles

Size D-3 (3.25 mm) crochet hook

Embroidery floss for mouth and eyes in colors of your choice

Tapestry, embroidery, and sewing needles

Invisible or brown sewing thread

Yarn scraps or fiberfill for stuffing

Safety pin

Other: brown felt, plastic eyes in the smallest size available or beads for eyes (optional), small bell

BODY

Using brown yarn, CO 22 sts. Place sts onto 3 dpns and join.

Rnds 1–6: Knit.

Rnd 7: Ssk at beg of rnd, K18, K2tog at end of rnd—20 sts.

Rnd 8: Knit.

Rnd 9: Ssk at beg of rnd, K16, K2tog at end of rnd—18 sts.

Back: Put 18 sts on 2 needles. Hold them parallel and with separate piece of brown yarn, weave the first 4 sts tog with the last 4 sts using Kitchener st (page 12).

Neck: Put the remaining 10 sts on 3 needles and knit 6 rnds.

Next rnd: K4, knit next 2 sts and put them on holder (safety pin), knit last 4 sts and first 4 sts again. Put these 8 sts on 1 needle for head.

HEAD

Row 1: P7, turn.

Row 2: YO, K6, turn.

Row 3: YO, P5, turn.

Row 4: YO, K4, turn.

Row 5: YO, P3, turn.

Row 6: YO, K2, turn.

Row 7: YO, purl to first YO, purl YO tog with next st, turn.

Row 8: Sl first st kw, knit to first YO, knit YO tog with next st, turn.

Row 9: Sl first st pw, purl to first YO, purl YO tog with next st, turn.

Rep rows 8 and 9 until all YOs have been worked. End with RS row.

Redistribute 8 sts onto 2 needles, place 2 sts from holder onto needle, and knit them. Knit next 4 sts. You have now completed a full rnd (10 sts) and you are back on top of reindeer's head.

Knit 3 rnds.

Next rnd: K2, ssk, K2, K2tog, K2—8 sts.

Change to beige yarn for muzzle/mouth.

Next rnd: Knit.

Next rnd: K3, K2tog, K3—7 sts.

Knit 1 more rnd. Gather and tie off, leaving 12" to pull back through head for a little stuffing.

Face: Using tapestry needle and red yarn, make large French knot for nose. Glue on eyes, make them with embroidery floss, or sew on small beads.

Ears: Cut ears of brown felt (pattern on page 25). Pinch ends and tack in place on sides of head using sewing needle and thread.

Tail: Attach brown yarn at top of back end with crochet hook. Ch 4, turn, sl st in second ch from hook and in next 2 chs. Tie off.

Antlers: Attach single strand of white yarn from inside of head with crochet hook. Ch 6, thread yarn back through chs and then through to location for next antler. Work second antler next to first.

Accessory: Tie a small bell on neck with strand of red yarn.

Reindeer's ear

Penguin

SUPPLIES

Black worsted-weight yarn (4)

Size 1 (2.25 mm) double-pointed needles

White, black, and gold or orange felt

Black beads or small glue-on eyes and craft glue

Tapestry, embroidery, and sewing needles

Invisible or white, black, and orange sewing thread

Yarn scraps or fiberfill for stuffing

BODY AND HEAD

This little penguin has an hourglass figure. You start with just 15 sts, inc to 19 at the middle, dec again for the neck, and then inc again for a little round head.

CO 15 sts. Place sts onto 3 dpns and join.

Rnds 1–5: Knit.

Rnd 6: K2, M1R, K4, M1L, K9—17 sts.

Rnds 7–9, 11–13, 15, 17, 18, and 20–24: Knit.

Rnd 10: K12, M1R, K3, M1L, K2—19.

Rnd 14: K1, ssk, K4, K2tog, K2, ssk, K3, K2tog, K1—15 sts.

Rnd 16: K1, ssk, K2, K2tog, K2, ssk, K1, K2tog, K1—11 sts.

Rnd 19: K2, M1R, K1, M1L, K5, M1R, K3—14 sts.

Rnd 25: Knit.

Gather and tie off.

FINISHING

Cut out piece of white felt using pattern (below). Using needle and white thread, make small, invisible sts between back of felt and top of black knit to attach felt to front of penguin.

Eyes: Glue on plastic eyes or sew on beads for eyes.

Beak and feet: Cut out pieces of orange felt for beak and feet using patterns (below). Pinch beak in half and tack to face. Use orange thread to tack feet to bottom edge of puppet.

Wings: Cut out pieces of black felt for wings using patterns (below). Use black thread to tack wings to sides of body.

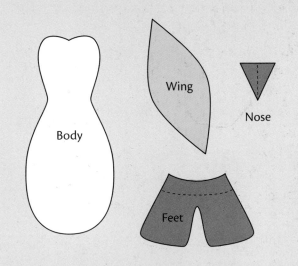

Wing

Nose

Body

Feet

Teddy Bear

SUPPLIES

Brown worsted-weight yarn (4)

Size 1 (2.25 mm) double-pointed needles

Size D-3 (3.25 mm) and C-2 (2.75 mm) crochet hooks

Black or pink embroidery floss

Tapestry, embroidery, and sewing needles

Invisible or brown sewing thread

Yarn scraps or fiberfill for stuffing

Other: small pieces of thick felt for nose and paws, black beads for eyes, red ribbon (optional)

BODY

Using brown yarn, CO 12 sts. Place sts onto 3 dpns and join.

Rnds 1–10: Knit.

Gather at top and leave 6" for attaching to head.

Paws: Attach 36" of brown yarn to one side of body for arms. Make st and then, using crochet hook, ch 6, turn, and sl into the second ch from hook and 4 remaining sts. Pull yarn through to other side and rep. If desired, cut out a ¼" circle of felt

and sew onto end of each paw with invisible sts. Repeat for legs.

Optional tummy: Cut a ⅝" circle of felt and st it in place with invisible sts between felt and yarn.

HEAD

Using brown yarn, CO 12 sts. Place sts onto 3 dpns and join.

Rnds 1–9: Knit.

Gather and tie off at top. Stuff lightly. Gather at bottom and leave 6" for attaching to body.

Attach head to body: Pull yarn ends back and forth through head and body and then, using sewing needle and thread, attach head to body with small sts.

Ears: Using brown yarn and tapestry needle, make small knots for ears, or using crochet hook, ch 2, tie off, pull through to other side, and rep.

FINISHING

Tail: Attach 12" of brown yarn to center of back. With smaller crochet hook, ch 4, tie off, and sew into circle.

Snout: Cut out a ¾" felt circle. With sewing needle and thread, run gathering sts around outside. Stuff with small amount of yarn to create a little snout and attach to face with invisible sts.

Eyes: With sewing needle and thread, tack black beads just above snout.

Nose and mouth: With sewing needle and thread, tack small black bead to top of snout. With embroidery needle and black or pink floss, embroider a wide mouth and a line between nose and mouth.

Accessory: If desired, tie a strand of red ribbon around neck.

Toy Car

My grandsons asked me if I could make some car puppets. I couldn't picture how I'd do it until my daughter-in-law held up an unfinished puppet body in a horizontal position—then we could all see the possibilities. The boys reached into the yarn basket and came up with every possible color of car— suddenly we were in the car business. This pattern has a spoiler.

SUPPLIES

Blue, white, and black worsted-weight yarn
Size 1 (2.25 mm) double-pointed needles
Size D-3 (3.25 mm) crochet hook
Silver metallic embroidery floss
Tapestry, embroidery, and sewing needles
Invisible or blue sewing thread
Other: white felt, 2 silver sequins (optional)

BODY

CO 12 sts. Place sts onto 3 dpns and join.

Hood

Rnds 1–6, 8, and 10–18: Knit.
Rnd 7: K5, M1R, K2, M1L, K5—14 sts.
Rnd 9: K5, M1R, K4, M1L, K5—16 sts.

Spoiler

Rnd 19: K12, BO last 4 sts of this rnd—12 sts rem.
Rnd 20: BO first 4 sts of this rnd, knit rem 8 sts.
Rnds 21 and 23: Purl.
Rnd 22: Knit.
BO.

   The back of the car always seems uneven to me so I cut off the yarn, leaving about a foot, and take some stitches around the back of the spoiler to even it out.

Tires

Mark spots for 4 wheels on sides of car. Attach black yarn to front wheel marker with crochet hook. Ch 6, make a circle, and tie off. With sewing needle and thread, invisibly attach wheel to car body at top and bottom.

Rep at other 3 markers.

With tapestry needle and white yarn, make a French knot in the middle of each tire—whitewalls!

ACCESSORIES

Windshield: Cut out a small rectangle of white felt, and with sewing needle and thread, st it in place. With embroidery needle and floss, outline windshield with metallic floss.

Headlights: Using embroidery needle and silver metallic floss, make a large French knot for each light. **Or,** with sewing needle and thread, st sequins to front of car.

The circus collection offers many opportunities for creativity. Clowns have so many different faces, body shapes, and hairstyles that they could be a whole collection of their own. Once you have completed one elephant, you can make an entire parade of them, tail to trunk, each with unique accessories.

Skill level: Cording for Trapeze Lady's legs, Elephant's trunk, and Giraffe's neck are **Experienced.** ◀■■■▷

All the others are **Easy.** ◀■■□▷

Ringmaster

SUPPLIES

Black, white, pink (or color of choice for skin), and red worsted-weight yarn (4)

Size 1 (2.25 mm) double-pointed needles

Size D-3 (3.25 mm) crochet hook

Tapestry, embroidery, and sewing needles

Invisible or pink sewing thread

Yarn scraps or fiberfill for stuffing

Embroidery floss for eyes and mouth in the colors of your choice

Other: red felt, 1 red or black bead for coat button

BODY

With black, CO 16 sts. Place sts onto 3 dpns and join.

Rnds 1–9: Knit.

Change to white.

Rnds 10–18: Knit.

Put the 16 sts on 2 needles, hold them parallel, and weave sts tog with Kitchener st (page 12).

Arms: Attach 36" of red yarn to one side of body near top. Make st and then, using crochet hook, ch 9 sts. Turn and sl st in second ch and each ch back to body. Pull yarn through to other side and rep.

Hands: With crochet hook, pull a piece of pink yarn through first ch on arm. Knot it and fray ends for fingers.

HEAD

With pink, CO 12 sts. Place sts onto 3 dpns and join.

Rnds 1–11: Knit.

Gather at top, leaving 12" for ears and nose. Stuff lightly. Gather at bottom and leave 6" for attaching to body.

Ears: Using tail of yarn and tapestry needle, make a small loose st on one side of head; then make a second st over that st, pull it through, and rep on other side.

Nose: Make a large French knot with pink yarn.

Attach head to body: Pull yarn ends back and forth through head and body and then, using sewing needle and thread, attach head to body with small sts.

FINISHING

Hair: Using black yarn and tapestry needle, make running sts from the sides, back, and front to a side part.

Mustache: Using black yarn and tapestry needle, make a small st on each side of nose.

Eyes and mouth: With embroidery needle and floss, embroider small French knots for eyes and a small V for mouth.

Coat: Cut out pattern from red felt (below). Overlap sides and st in place with invisible sts. Sew a tiny bead in front.

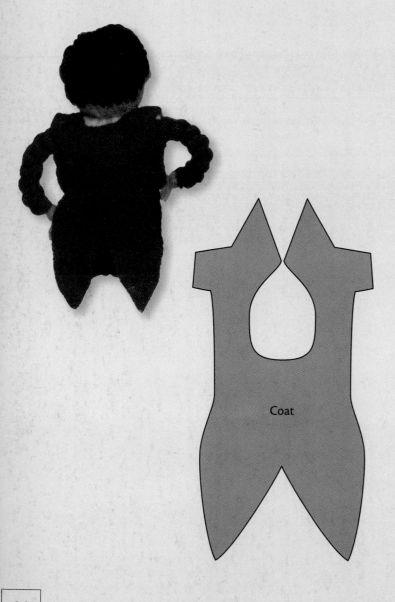

Coat

Trapeze Lady

SUPPLIES

Variegated, hot pink, brown, and pink (or color of choice for skin) worsted-weight yarn (4)

Size 1 (2.25 mm) double-pointed needles

Size D-3 (3.25 mm) crochet hook

Embroidery floss for mouth and eyes in colors of your choice

Tapestry, embroidery, and sewing needles

Invisible or pink sewing thread

Yarn scraps or fiberfill for stuffing

Other: beads for earrings; scrap of hot pink felt for slippers; lace, pearls, and feathers to embellish costume; metallic embroidery floss for hair ornament; small paper umbrella (all optional)

BODY

With variegated yarn, CO 16 sts. Place sts onto 3 dpns and join.

Rnds 1 and 2: Purl.

Rnds 3–8, 10–12, and 14–17: Knit.

Rnd 9: K1, ssk, K2, K2tog, knit to end of rnd—14 sts.

Rnd 13 (inc rnd): K2, M1R, K2, M1L, knit to end of rnd—16 sts.

Place sts onto 2 needles. Hold the needles parallel and weave sts tog using Kitchener st (page 12).

Thread yarn back through to other side when you have removed last st. This will help to make the shoulders look even.

Arms: Attach 36" of pink yarn at one side of body. Make st and then, using crochet hook, ch 10 sts. Turn, sl st into second ch from hook and into next 8 sts. Attach and rep on other side for second arm.

HEAD

With pink, CO 10 sts. Place sts onto 3 dpns and join.

Rnds 1–9: Knit.

Gather and tie off at top, leaving 12" for nose and ears.

Stuff lightly and gather at bottom, leaving 6" for attaching to body.

Face: Using embroidery needle and floss, embroider eyes and a smile. Using yarn tail and tapestry needle, make small French knots at each side for ears and one in the middle of her face for nose. If desired, use sewing needle and thread to tack on beads for earrings.

Hair: Using brown yarn and tapestry needle, make long sts on front, sides, and back to the top of head. Then make loose sts of yarn at the top of head to make curls.

If desired, add a crown of metallic thread or gold lace or a headdress made from tiny feathers or jewels.

Attach head to body: Pull yarn end back and forth through head and body and then, using sewing needle and thread, attach head to body with small sts.

LEGS

In the past I have just used single chaining with double thread, but this I-cord technique gives a better look for the long legs of a girl on a trapeze. (Try a sample of both first.)

Mark the middle of CO rnd of body and pin a length of pink yarn, about 36" long, in place with half on each side. Using this piece of yarn, pick up 3 sts along CO rnd with a dpn. Knit those 3 sts, then push sts to other end of needle and knit them again. Pull yarn tight because you are really creating a circle. Continue in this way for 10 rnds. Cut pink yarn.

Slippers: Carefully tie on hot pink yarn and continue cording for 2 more rnds. Gather 3 sts, tie off, pull yarn up through the leg a few sts to hide end, and cut. If desired, wrap a tiny bit of felt around bottom of foot and st in place. Rep for second leg.

Clowns

SUPPLIES

White, orange, blue, red, and varie-gated worsted-weight yarn

Size 1 (2.25 mm) double-pointed needles

Size D-3 (3.25 mm) crochet hook

Tapestry, embroidery, and sewing needles

Invisible or white sewing thread

Yarn scraps or fiberfill for stuffing

Embroidery floss for eyes and mouth in colors of your choice

Other: 2 small stitch markers for juggling rings, gold felt, 2 beads for suspender buttons (optional)

BODY

Using variegated or solid-colored color yarn, CO 16 sts. Place sts onto 3 dpns and join.

Rnds 1–12: Knit.

Rnd 13: Purl.

Change to any contrasting yarn.

Rnds 14–21: Knit.

Gather sts and tie off.

Arms: Join 36" of variegated or solid-colored yarn at side of body. Make st and then, using crochet hook, ch 12 sts. Turn, sl st in second st from hook and in each of remaining sts. Pull yarn through to other side and rep.

Suspenders: With crochet hook, ch 24–28 sts and tie off. Attach at front and back on top of purl rnd. If desired, use sewing needle and thread to tack on beads for suspender buttons.

HEAD

Using white yarn, CO 12 sts. Place sts onto 3 dpns and join.

Rnds 1–12: Knit.

Gather and tie off at top, leaving 12" for ears. Stuff lightly. Gather at bottom and leave 6" for attaching to body.

Face: With embroidery needle and floss, st eyes, mouth, and big glasses—or what-ever comes to mind—to personalize your clown.

Ears: With white yarn and tapestry needle, on each side of head make small or large French knots for ears.

Nose: With red yarn and tapestry needle, make a large French knot.

Attach head to body: Pull yarn ends back and forth through head and body and then, using sewing needle and thread, attach head to body with small sts.

Hair: With orange yarn and tapestry needle make small, very loose sts of hair on sides and top of head. Or create a unique hairstyle of your own (page 62).

FINISHING

Bow tie: Cut tie from gold felt and use sewing needle and thread to tack in place (see pattern below).

Feet: Cut feet from gold felt and use sewing needle and thread attach to front of CO rnd as marked on the pattern (below).

Juggling rings: Use white yarn to tack a st marker to the end of each arm.

Bow tie

Foot

Baby and Mother Monkeys

A monkey was one of the very first puppets I ever made. Each one has its own personality and look. Some have longer tails or bigger noses, and I've made them in many colors. In these patterns there are some decreases in the back to give both monkeys some shape. With only nine stitches and nine rounds, you can create a whole jungle full of these in a very short time.

SUPPLIES

Dark brown worsted-weight yarn (4)

Size 1 (2.25 mm) double-pointed needles

Size D-3 (3.25 mm) crochet hook

Tapestry, embroidery, and sewing needles

Invisible or brown sewing thread

Yarn scraps or fiberfill for stuffing

Embroidery floss in black or brown and pink or beige

Other: tan or beige felt

BABY MONKEY

Body

CO14 sts. Place sts onto 3 dpns and join.

Rnds 1–3, 5, and 7–9: Knit.

Rnd 4: Ssk, K10, K2tog—12 sts.

Rnd 6: Ssk, K8, K2tog—10 sts.

Gather and tie off. Leave a 6" tail for attaching to head.

Arms: Attach 36" of brown yarn at shoulder. Make st and then, using crochet hook, ch 9 sts. Turn, sl st into 2nd ch from hook and into next 7 sts. Pull yarn through and rep on other side for second arm.

Belly: Cut an oval piece of felt that matches face and use sewing needle and thread to st it to front of the monkey with small, invisible sts.

Legs: Attach 36" of brown yarn at bottom of body. Make st and then, using crochet hook, ch 10. Turn, and sl st into second ch from hook and next 7 chs. Pull through to other side and rep for second leg.

Tail: Attach 16" of brown yarn to center back. Make a st and then, using crochet hook, ch 10 and tie off. St middle of tail to middle of back to make a little curl.

Head

CO 9 sts. Place sts onto 3 dpns and join.

Rnds 1–5 and 7–8: Knit.

Rnd 6: K7, M1, K2—10 sts.

Gather and tie off, leaving 12" to make loops for ears. Stuff lightly. Gather at bottom, leaving 6" for attaching to body.

Ears: Pull yarn through to one side of head. With crochet hook, ch 2, tie off, pull through to other side, and rep. Using embroidery needle and floss, make a small pink or beige French knot in center of each ear. Pull end into head.

Attach head to body: Pull yarn ends back and forth through head and body and then, using sewing needle and thread, attach head to body with small sts.

Face

Cut a 1" circle of tan or beige felt.

Using sewing needle and thread, carefully run a gathering thread around outside of felt. Place a small bit of stuffing or some leftover yarn in center, then pull thread gently until it draws in the felt to create a ball. With invisible sts, sew it to head near bottom of face.

Eyes: Using pattern (page 34), cut a piece of felt for eye area. Use sewing needle and thread with invisible sts to attach it to face. With embroidery needle and black or brown floss, make small French knots for eyes.

Mouth and nose: With embroidery needle and black or brown floss, embroider a mouth and make a small knot for nose.

MOTHER MONKEY

Body

CO 16 sts. Place sts onto 3 dpns and join.

Rnds 1–3, 5, and 7–14: Knit.

Rnd 4: Ssk, K12, K2tog—14 sts.

Rnd 6: Ssk, K10, K2tog—12 sts.

Gather and tie off. Leave a 6" tail for attaching head to body.

Arms: Attach 36" of brown yarn at shoulder. Make st and then, using crochet hook, ch 10 sts. Turn and sl st into second ch from hook and next 8 chs. Pull through to other side and rep for second arm.

Belly: Cut an oval piece of felt that matches face and use sewing needle and thread to st it to front of the monkey with small, invisible sts.

Legs: Attach 36" of brown yarn at bottom. Make st and then, using crochet hook, ch 11 sts. Turn and sl st into second ch from hook and next 9 chs. Attach to body and rep on other side. The legs and arms will curl slightly.

Tail: Ch 12 and tie off. St middle of tail to middle of back to make a little curl.

Head

CO 11 sts. Place sts onto 3 dpns and join.

Knit 9 rnds.

Gather and tie off, leaving 12" to make loops for ears. Stuff lightly. Gather at bottom and leave 6" for attaching to body.

Ears: Pull yarn through to one side of head. With crochet hook, ch 3, tie off, pull yarn through to other side and rep. Using embroidery needle and pink or beige floss, make a small French knot in center of each ear.

Attach head to body: Pull yarn ends back and forth through head and body and then, using sewing needle and thread, attach head to body with small sts.

Face

Cut a 1¼" felt circle. Create face and join it as for Baby Monkey (page 33).

Eyes and nose: Using pattern below, and with embroidery needle and black or brown floss, make small French knots for eyes.

Mouth: Use black embroidery floss for mouth.

Mother monkey eyes

Baby monkey eyes

Tiger

SUPPLIES

Black, orange, and white worsted-weight yarn [4]

Size 1 (2.25 mm) double-pointed needles

Size D-3 (3.25 mm) crochet hook

Tapestry, embroidery, and sewing needles

Invisible or orange sewing thread

Yarn scraps or fiberfill for stuffing

Black embroidery floss

Other: black or gold beads (optional)

BODY

With orange, CO 15 sts. Place sts onto 3 dpns and join. Tie on black.

Knit 16 rnds, working odd-numbered rnds in orange and even-numbered rnds in black.

Gather and tie off. Leave 6" tail for attaching head to body.

Arms: Attach 1 strand of black and 1 strand of orange, 36" long, at one side of body. With both strands of yarn held tog and crochet hook, ch 5. Turn, sl st into second ch from hook and next 3 chs. Pull yarn through and rep on other side.

HEAD

Using orange yarn, CO 15 sts. Place sts onto 3 dpns and join.

Rnds 1 and 2: Knit.

Rnd 3: Tie on black and knit.

Knit odd-numbered rnds in black and even-numbered rnds in orange.

Rnd 4: With orange, K4, pick up the yarn between the 4th and 5th st and knit (M1), K to end of rnd—16 sts.

Rnds 5, 7, and 9: With black, knit.

Rnd 6: With orange, K3, M1R, K3, M1L, K6, M1R, K1, M1L, K3—20 sts.

Rnd 8: With orange, K3, ssk, K1, K2tog, knit to end of rnd—18 sts.

Rnd 10: With orange, K2, ssk, K1, K2tog, K4, ssk, K1, K2tog, K2—14 sts.

Rnd 11: Knit.

Place sts evenly on 2 needles, hold them parallel, and weave sts tog using Kitchener st (page 12), leaving 18" to crochet ears.

Ears: With tail of orange, make loop with crochet hook, ch 4 and attach close to first ch st. Pull yarn through to other side and rep.

Gather at bottom, leaving 6" for attaching to body.

Attach head to body: Pull yarn ends back and forth through head and body and then, using sewing needle and thread, attach head to body with small sts.

Muzzle: Using white yarn and tapestry needle, make several long horizontal sts across bottom of face. Gather these tog with 1 vertical st in center. Tie a small piece of white yarn below muzzle for a little beard.

Eyes and nose: With embroidery needle and black floss, st nose and eyes; or use sewing needle and thread to attach small black or gold beads for eyes.

Tail: Attach 12" length of black yarn at center of back on bottom. Make st and ch 8 or 9 with crochet hook. Tie off leaving enough to fray ends a little. St tail to back with needle and thread to make a little curl.

Lion

SUPPLIES

Light gold, dark gold, and white worsted-weight yarn (4)

Size 1 (2.25 mm) double-pointed needles

Size D-3 (3.25 mm) crochet hook

Brown embroidery floss for nose and eyes

Tapestry, embroidery, and sewing needles

Invisible or light gold sewing thread

Yarn scraps or fiberfill for stuffing

Other: beads for eyes (optional)

BODY

Using light gold yarn, CO 15 sts. Place sts onto 3 dpns and join.

Rnds 1–9: Knit.

Rnds 10–17: Purl.

Gather and tie off. Leave 6" tail for attaching head to body.

Arms: Join 2 strands of light gold yarn, 36" long, at shoulder. Make st and then, using crochet hook, ch 6 sts. Turn, sl st into second ch from hook and next 4 sts. Attach and rep on other side for second arm.

Tail: Attach 12" length of matching yarn at center of back on bottom. Make st and ch 8 or 9 with crochet hook. Tie off leaving enough to fray ends a little. St tail to back with needle and thread to make a little curl.

HEAD

Most of the shaping on the head occurs at the front of the face, but a few rows have shaping for the back of the head. The notes below will help you keep track of the front and the back.

Using light gold, CO 12 sts. Place sts onto 3 dpns and join.

Rnds 1, 3, 5, and 9: Knit.

Rnd 2: K5, M1R, K2, M1L, K5—14 sts.

Rnd 4: K5, M1R, K4, M1L, K5—16 sts.

Rnd 6: K5, M1R, K6, M1L, K5—18 sts.

Rnd 7 (shape back of head): K3, M1L, K12, M1R, K3—20 sts.

Rnd 8: K5, ssk, K6, k2tog, K5—18 sts.

Rnd 10: K5, ssk, K4, K2tog K5—16 sts.

Rnd 11 (shape back of head): K1, K2tog, K10, ssk, K1—14 sts.

Rnd 12: K5 ssk, K2tog, K5—12 sts.

Rnd 13: Knit.

Knit 3 sts from next rnd, then arrange sts on 2 dpns with 6 sts on each needle, making sure to have front sts on 1 needle and the back sts on 2nd needle. Weave tog using Kitchener st (page 12).

Gather and tie off at top. Stuff lightly and gather at bottom.

Attach head to body: Pull yarn ends back and forth through head and body and then, using sewing needle and thread, attach head to body with small sts.

FACE

Snout: With tapestry needle and white yarn, make horizontal sts along center of face in shape of a snout.

Eyes: With embroidery needle and brown floss, make small knots for eyes or with sewing needle and thread, sew beads on for eyes.

Mouth: With embroidery needle and brown floss, st mouth.

Mane: With dark gold yarn and tapestry needle, make small, loopy sts around face. Do not pull sts tight.

Giraffe

I've never found a yarn that is just right for making giraffe spots, and I don't think that it makes sense to try to make the spots by changing yarn colors in such a small project. I have several solutions: one is to use a brown permanent marker and draw a few free-form shapes on each giraffe side. I've also embroidered spots using dark gold embroidery floss, making short stitches in an uneven pattern all over the body. Another plan is just to use solid dark gold yarn and let children imagine the spots.

SUPPLIES

Gold and brown worsted-weight yarn 4

Size 1 (2.25 mm) double-pointed needles

Size D-3 (3.25 mm) crochet hook

Tapestry, embroidery, and sewing needles

Yarn scraps or fiberfill for stuffing

Dark brown and dark gold embroidery floss for nose, eyes, and spots

Safety pin

Craft glue (optional)

Other: small plastic eyes (optional)

BODY

Using gold yarn, CO 17 sts, leaving 6" tail for making puppet tail later. Place sts onto 3 dpns and join.

Rnds 1–5, 7, 9, 11: Knit.

Rnd 6: K1, ssk, K11, K2tog, K1—15 sts.

Rnd 8: K1, ssk, K9, K2tog, K1—13 sts.

Rnd 10: K1, ssk, K7, K2tog, K1—11 sts.

Rnd 12: K1, ssk, K5, K2tog, K1—9 sts.

Rnds 13–19: Knit.

K3, knit next 3 sts, put them on holder (safety pin), knit last 3 sts of rnd, and then knit first 3 sts again. You will now be working just on these 6 sts until curve of head is complete. Place all 6 sts on 1 needle and turn.

HEAD

Row 1: P5, turn.

Row 2: YO, K4, turn.

Row 3: YO, P3, turn.

Row 4: YO, K2, turn.

Row 5: YO, purl to first YO, purl YO tog with next st, turn.

Row 6: Sl first st kw, knit to first YO, knit YO tog with next st, turn.

Row 7: Sl first st pw, purl to first YO, purl YO tog with next st, turn.

Rep rows 6 and 7 until all YOs have been worked.

You should end with a knit side and 6 sts. Place sts onto 2 needles. End after working a knit row.

FACE

Return to working in the rnd. K3 sts from needle 1, K3 sts from holder, K3 sts from needle 3. You now have 9 sts on 3 needles.

Rnds 1 and 2: Knit.

Rnd 3: K2, ssk, K1, K2tog, K2—7 sts.

Rnd 4: Knit.

Rnd 5: K1, ssk, K1, K2tog, K1—5 sts.

Gather and tie off at top. Pull yarn back through head to hide end.

Ears: Giraffe ears stick out from their heads. Mark with pins where you'd like the ears to be. To make yarn ears: with matching yarn, sc 2 sts with smaller crochet hook. Knot it and pull yarn through to other side and rep. To make felted ears: cut 2 very small triangles—about ½" long—out of matching or contrasting felt. Fold each ear in half and tack in place with tiny sts on sides of head.

Eyes: With embroidery needle and floss, embroider large brown eyes or glue small plastic eyes in place.

Nose: With sewing needle and thread, make some small invisible sts around inside of snout for more definition, if desired. With embroidery needle and floss, make a small knot for nose.

FINISHING

Spots: With tapestry needle and dark gold floss, make short sts in uneven pattern on body and neck for spots.

Mane: With brown yarn and tapestry needle, make very loose sts down center of back.

Tail: Pull yarn from beg of CO through to the place where you want tail to begin. Ch 3 or 4, tie off, and slightly fray ends.

Optional horns: Mark 2 places with pins on top of head. Pull matching or contrasting yarn through 1 of these places, make a loop, and sc 3 or 4 sts. Pull yarn back through chain to other marked place. Rep for other horn.

Elephant

SUPPLIES

Gray worsted-weight yarn (4)

Size 1 (2.25 mm) double-pointed needles

Size D-3 (3.25 mm) crochet hook

Embroidery floss for nose and eyes in the colors of your choice

Tapestry, embroidery, and sewing needles

Invisible or gray sewing thread

Yarn scraps or fiberfill for stuffing

Other: red and gray felt, gold lace or rickrack, small beads in assorted colors to accessorize your elephant, black beads for eyes (optional)

BODY AND HEAD

CO 27 sts. Distribute onto 3 dpn and knit 7 rnds.

Rnds 8 through 14 will shape the back.

Rnd 8: K1, ssk, K21, K2tog, K1—25 sts.

Rnd 9: K1, ssk, K19, K2tog, K1—23 sts.

Rnd 10: K1, ssk, K17, K2tog, K1—21 sts.

Rnd 11: K1, ssk, K15, K2tog, K1—19 sts.

Rnd 12: K1, ssk, K13, K2tog, K1—17 sts.

Rnd 13: K1, ssk, K11, K2tog, K1—15 sts.

Rnd 14: K1, ssk, K9, K2tog, K1—13 sts.

Rnd 15: K4 from needle 1, knit the next 5 sts and put these 5 on holder, knit to end of rnd.

Knit 4 from needle 1 once more. Place these 8 sts on 1 needle, turn and beg to work gusset for head.

Row 1: Purl 7 and turn.

Row 2: YO, K6, turn.

Row 3: YO, P5, turn.

Row 4: YO, K4, turn.

Row 5: YO, P3, turn.

Row 6: YO, K2, turn.

Row 7: YO, purl to the first YO, purl YO tog with next st, turn.

Row 8: Sl 1, knit to next YO, knit YO tog with next st, turn.

Row 9: Sl 1, purl to next YO, purl YO tog with next st, turn.

Rep rows 8 and 9 until all YOs have been worked. End after working a knit row.

Divide the 8 sts onto 2 needles. Pick up the 5 sts from holder and knit to end of rnd.

Next rnd: Knit 1 rnd—13 sts.

Next rnd: K2, K2tog, K5, ssk, K2—11 sts.

Next rnd: K1, K2tog, ssk, K1, K2tog, ssk, K1—7 sts.

Next rnd: K2, BO 3, K2—4 sts.

Then K2 from needle 1.

Trunk: Place remaining 4 sts on 1 needle and work I-cord (page 13) until trunk is approx 1" long or desired length.

BO all sts and weave yarn end back into trunk.

Loosely stuff head with leftover yarn.

Finishing: Cut a small rectangle of red felt for blanket and place it over back (pattern below). St rickrack or lace around edges to hold in place. If desired, string beads around top of head for a crown.

Tail: Pull yarn from beginning of CO up to back. Ch 3 or 4, tie off and slightly fray edges of tail.

Eyes: With embroidery needle and floss, make small French knots; or with sewing needle and thread, sew on beads for eyes.

Ears: Cut gray felt using ear pattern (below). With sewing needle and thread, use invisible sts to tack ears to sides of head.

Crown: String some small beads and sew onto top of head.

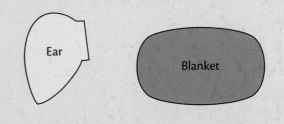

Ear

Blanket

The Enchanted Forest

The Three Little Pigs, Goldilocks and the family of bears, Little Red Riding Hood, and Cinderella are all enjoying a lovely day in the forest. Peeking out from behind the trees are witches, wolves, wizards, and dragons. Except for the dragon, the puppets in this section are relatively simple to make. The human characters have basic round heads and basic body shapes. The animal heads have some increases and decreases to create snouts or noses. The witch and the wizard both have robe-shaped bodies. Once you've made a few of the characters in this forest, you'll see the puppet possibilities in all your favorite childhood stories.

Skill Levels: The dragon's head shaping classifies him as **Experienced.** ◼◼◼◼
All the others are **Easy** ◼◼◻◻ because they require increases, decreases, and a variety of stitches.

Wizard

SUPPLIES

Gold, white, and pink (or color of choice for skin) worsted-weight yarns (4)

Size 1 (2.25 mm) double-pointed needles

Size D-3 (3.25 mm) crochet hook

Tapestry, embroidery, and sewing needles

Invisible or pink and black sewing thread

Yarn scraps or fiberfill for stuffing

Straight pins

Embroidery floss for mouth and eyes in the colors of your choice

Craft glue (optional)

Other: black felt, gold pipe cleaner, stars for hat (optional), miniature vessel to carry

BODY

Using gold yarn, CO 28 sts. Place sts onto 3 dpns and join.

Rnd 1: Purl.

Rnds 2 and 3: Knit.

Rnd 4: K12, K2tog, K12, K2tog—26 sts.

Rnds 5 and 6: Knit.

Continue to dec every 3rd rnd as foll, working 2 rnds even between each dec rnd:

Rnd 7: K11, K2tog, K11, K2tog—24 sts.

Rnd 10: K10, K2tog, K10, K2tog—22 sts.

Rnd 13: K9, K2tog, K9, K2tog—20 sts.

Rnd 16: K8, K2tog, K8, K2tog—18 sts.

Rnd 19: K7, K2tog, K7, K2tog—16 sts.

Rnd 22: K6, K2tog, K6, K2tog—14 sts.

Rnd 25: K5, K2tog, K5, K2tog—12 sts.

Rnd 26: Knit.

Gather and tie off. Leave a 6" tail for attaching head to body.

Arms: Attach 2 strands of gold yarn, 36" long, at one side of body. Holding strands tog, make st and then, using crochet hook, ch 10 sts. Turn and sl st into 2nd ch and rem 8 chs. Pull through to other side and rep.

HEAD

With pink yarn, CO 12 sts. Place sts onto 3 dpns and join.

Rnds 1–11: Knit.

Gather and tie off at top, leaving 12" for ears and nose. Stuff lightly and gather at bottom, leaving 6" tail for attaching to body.

Nose and ears: With yarn tail and tapestry needle, make small French knots for ears on each side and a double knot for nose.

Attach head to body: Pull yarn ends back and forth through head and body and then, using sewing needle and thread, attach head to body with small sts.

Beard and mustache: Cut 10 pieces of white yarn into 4" lengths. Lay them flat and parallel and run a white thread through middle of all of them. Fold the lengths in half at thread line. Pin beard to face from one ear to the other and st in place with invisible sts. Make two small sts in white yarn for mustache under nose.

Hair: Since you will be covering most of the head with the hat, just take a few long sts with white yarn around bottom of head and one st in front of each ear.

Mouth and eyes: With embroidery needle and floss, st a little curve for mouth and make 2 French knots for eyes.

Hat: Cut half of a 4" diameter circle (pattern below) and wrap it into a cone. St tog along the overlap. To get that little curve at the top, pull sts tight and secure with a knot. Any color of hat will do, but I love this black felt with glitter on it. If you can't find that, glue some small stars all over the hat.

ACCESSORIES

The wizard's staff is a gold pipe cleaner that I folded into a star at top in one continuous line (see the illustration below). With sewing needle and thread, tack staff into one of the hands.

The wizard also carries a pot of secret potions. Many craft stores have great collections of miniatures. Leave the pot in the original finish or paint it with shiny paints. Sew or glue the vessel into other hand.

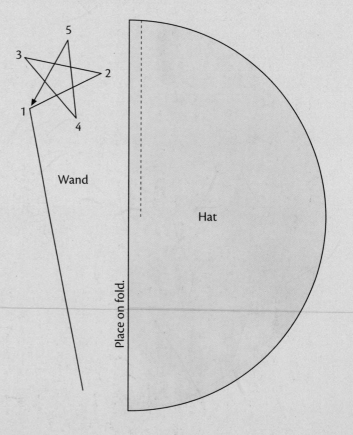

Wand

Hat

Place on fold.

Fire-Breathing Dragon

SUPPLIES

Green and variegated worsted-weight yarn

4

Size 1 (2.25) double-pointed needles

Size D-3 (3.25 mm) crochet hook

Yellow embroidery floss for eyes

Tapestry, embroidery, and sewing needles

Invisible or green sewing thread

Yarn scraps or fiberfill for stuffing

Yellow and orange felt

Red beads for eyes

BODY

Using green yarn, CO 20 sts. Place sts onto 3 dpns and join. Work 8 rows in seed st as foll:

Rnd 1: (K1, P1) around.

Rnd 2: (P1, P1) around.

Rnds 3–8: Work rnds 1 and 2 another 3 times.

Rnds 9–11, 13, 15, and 17–25: Knit.

Rnd 12: K1, ssk, K14, K2tog, K1—18 sts.

Rnd 14: K1, ssk, K12, K2tog, K1—16 sts.

Rnd 16: K1, ssk, K10, K2tog, K1—14 sts.

Rnd 26: K1, ssk, K8, K2tog, K1—12 sts.

BO.

HEAD

Using green yarn, CO 14 sts. Place sts onto 3 dpns and join.

Rnds 1–8: Work in seed st as for body.

Rnd 9: K4, ssk, K2, K2tog, K4—12 sts.

Rnds 10, 12, 14–16, and 18: Knit.

Rnd 11: K3, ssk, K2, K2tog, K3—10 sts.

Rnd 13: K2, ssk, K2, K2tog, K2—8 sts.

Rnd 17: K1, ssk, K2tog, ssk, K2tog, K1—6 sts.

Rnd 19: Ssk, K2, K2tog—4 sts.

Rnd 20: K2tog twice—2 sts.

Rnd 21: Knit.

BO 1 st. Do not tie off.

FINISHING

Horns: First make horn at end of snout. Using crochet hook, ch 6. Tie off and pull yarn back through chain and into head. Attach yarn to back of head to make 2 more horns.

Mane: With variegated yarn, ch 40 sts and tie off. Pin this piece on back to look like ridges, tucking end under bottom edge of body. St in place with sewing needle and thread.

Eyes: With embroidery needle and yellow floss, embroider eyes. With sewing needle and thread, attach a small red bead in each eye center.

Fire breath: Cut out fire from red and yellow felt (pattern below) and attach to mouth using sewing needle and thread, making invisible sts.

Connecting head and body: Pin head to body at an angle and attach it with sewing needle and thread, making invisible sts.

Sew head to body with invisible stitches.

Dragon's horns and mane   Dragon's fire

Hansel and Gretel

HANSEL

Supplies

Variegated, pink (or color of choice for skin), brown, and white worsted-weight yarn (**4**)

Size 1 (2.25 mm) double-pointed needles

Size D-3 (3.25 mm) crochet hook

Embroidery floss for eyes and mouth

Tapestry, embroidery, and sewing needles

Invisible or pink sewing thread

Yarn scraps or fiberfill for stuffing

Body

Using variegated yarn, CO 14 sts for the pants. Place sts onto 3 dpns and join.

Rnds 1–9: Knit.

Rnd 10: Purl.

Cut yarn. Tie on white yarn for shirt.

Rnds 11–19: Knit.

Gather and tie off. Leave 6" tail for attaching head to body.

Arms: Attach 36" of white yarn at one side of body. Make st and then, using crochet hook, ch 8. Turn, and sl st into second ch from hook and next 6 chs. Pull yarn through and rep on other side.

Hands: With crochet hook, pull a piece of pink yarn through first ch on arm. Knot it and fray ends for fingers.

Suspenders (make 2): With multicolored yarn and crochet hook, ch 25 and tie off. With sewing needle and thread, tack suspenders to front and back.

Head

Using pink yarn, CO 12 sts. Place sts onto 3 dpns and join.

Rnds 1–10: Knit.

Gather and tie off at top, leaving 12" for nose and ears. Stuff lightly. Gather at bottom and leave 6" for attaching to body.

Nose and ears: With yarn tail and tapestry needle, make small knots.

Eyes and mouth: With embroidery needle and floss, make small French knots for eyes and use straight sts to make a smiling mouth.

Hair: Using brown yarn and tapestry needle, make long sts across top of head. Bring yarn up at top of head and trim to make a cowlick. See "Hairstyles" (page 62) for more ideas.

Attach head to body: Pull yarn ends back and forth through head and body and then, using sewing needle and thread, attach head to body with small sts.

GRETEL

Supplies

Pink (or color of choice for skin), tan, and baby blue worsted-weight yarn (**4**)

Size 1 (2.25 mm) double-pointed needles

Size D-3 (3.25 mm) crochet hook

Embroidery yarn for eyes and mouth in the colors of your choice

Tapestry, embroidery, and sewing needles

Invisible or pink sewing thread

Yarn scraps or fiberfill for stuffing

Body

Using baby blue yarn, CO 14 sts. Place sts onto 3 dpns and join.

Rnds 1–8: (K1, P1) around.

Rnds 9–16: Knit.

Gather and tie off at top, leaving 6" for attaching head.

Arms: Attach 36" of matching yarn at one side of body. Make a st and then, using crochet hook, ch 8. Turn and sl st into second chain from hook and rem 6 chs. Pull yarn through and rep on other side.

Hands: With crochet hook, pull piece of pink yarn through first ch on arm. Knot it and fray ends for fingers.

Head

Using pink yarn, CO 12 sts. Place sts onto 3 dpns and join.

Rnds 1–10: Knit.

Gather and tie off at top, leaving 12" tail for nose and ears. Stuff lightly and gather at bottom, leaving 6" for attaching to body.

Nose and ears: With yarn tail and tapestry needle, make small knots.

Eyes and mouth: With embroidery needle and floss, make small French knots for eyes and use straight sts to make smiling mouth.

Finishing

Attach head to body: Pull yarn ends back and forth through head and body and then, using sewing needle and thread, attach head to body with small sts.

Hair: To make braids, cut pieces of tan yarn in 4" lengths. Lay them on a flat surface and carefully run a matching thread through middle of them using sewing needle. Lay hair on top of head with middle of yarn on middle of head. St in place at center; then braid and tack braids in place at sides.

Tie ends of braids with embroidery floss for decoration. If desired, add little sts at top in front for bangs.

Witch

SUPPLIES

Black and pink (or color of choice for skin) worsted-weight yarn (4)

Size 1 (2.25 mm) double-pointed needles

Size D-3 (3.25 mm) crochet hook

Embroidery yarn for eyes and mouth in the colors of your choice

Tapestry, embroidery, and sewing needles

Invisible or black sewing thread

Yarn scraps or fiberfill for stuffing

Black felt

BODY

Using black yarn, CO 24 sts. Place sts onto 3 dpns and join.

Rnds 1–6: Knit.

Rnd 7: (K2, ssk, K4, K2tog, K2) twice—20 sts.

Rnds 8 and 9: Knit.

Rnd 10: (K2, ssk, K2, K2tog, K2) twice—16 sts.

Rnd 11–24: Knit.

Gather and tie off. Leave a 6" tail for attaching head to body.

Arms: Attach 36" of black yarn to one side of body. Make st and then, using crochet hook, ch 9 sts. Turn and sl st into second ch and next 7 chs for long, slender arms. Pull yarn through and rep on other side.

HEAD

Using pink yarn, CO 12 sts. Place sts onto 3 dpns and join.

Rnds 1–12: Knit.

Gather and tie off at top, leaving 12" for nose and ears. Stuff lightly. Gather at bottom and leave 6" for attaching to the body.

Attach head to body: Pull yarn ends back and forth through head and body and then, using sewing needle and thread, attach head to body with small sts.

Nose: With pink yarn and tapestry needle, make a French knot; then make several sts around that knot to make a big, uneven nose.

Mouth and Eyes: With embroidery needle and floss, embroider a straight mouth and tiny eyes.

Hair: Cut ten 5" lengths of black yarn. Lay them on a flat surface and carefully run a black thread through middle of them. Then lay them across top of head. St them in place in middle with sewing needle and thread. Let hair be wild and uneven.

Hat: Use pattern for wizard hat (page 42) to cut out a piece of black felt. Overlap edges; then st straight sides tog to fit head. Gently stretch bottom of felt to create a brim. It will be a little uneven and that's good. Use sewing needle and thread to tack hat to head with invisible sts.

Cinderella

SUPPLIES

Blue, pink (or color of choice for skin), and gold worsted-weight yarn ⓸

Size 1 (2.25 mm) double-pointed needles

Size D-3 (3.25 mm) crochet hook

Embroidery floss for eyes and mouth in the colors of your choice

Tapestry, embroidery, and sewing needles

Invisible or pink sewing thread

Yarn scraps or fiberfill for stuffing

Other: metallic lace trim, beads for earrings (optional)

BODY

Using blue yarn, CO 22 sts. Place sts onto 3 dpns and join.

Rnds 1 and 2: Purl.

Rnds 3–5, 7, 9, 11, 13, 14, and 15: Knit.

Rnd 6: K1, ssk, K7, K2tog, K10—20 sts.

Rnd 8: K1, ssk, K5, K2tog, K10—18 sts.

Rnd 10: K1, ssk, K3, K2tog, K10—16 sts.

Rnd 12: K1, ssk, K1, K2tog, K2, ssk, K3, K2tog, K1—12 sts.

Rnd 16: K2, M1R, K1, M1L, K9—14 sts.

Rnd 17–19: Knit.

Put the rem 14 sts on 2 needles and weave tog using Kitchener st (page 12).

Arms: Attach 36" of pink yarn to one side of body. Make st and then, using crochet hook, ch 8 sts. Turn, sl st into second ch and next 6 sts. Pull through to other side and rep.

HEAD

Using pink yarn, CO 11 sts. Place sts onto 3 dpns and join.

Rnds 1–9: Knit.

Gather and tie off at top, leaving 12" for nose and ears. Stuff lightly. Gather at bottom and leave 6" for attaching to body.

Ears and nose: With pink yarn or embroidery floss, make small stitches for the ears and nose.

Eyes and mouth: With embroidery needle and floss, embroider eyes and mouth in any color you choose. Add eyebrows if you like.

Hair: With gold yarn, do long sts all over head from front, back, and sides up to top. Then make a large knot of matching worsted and st it to center of head.

Earrings: Use sewing needle and thread to tack on small beads for earrings.

FINISHING

Attach head to body: Pull yarn ends back and forth through head and body and then, using sewing needle and thread, attach head to body with small sts.

Adding details: The trim on the front of Cinderella's gown is a piece of silver lace. I have also used gold thread or yarn. Use the same for a small crown. Or, you may want to leave off the trim and add beads or other jewelry. It's up to you. Sew the trim on with the sewing needle and thread.

The Prince

SUPPLIES

Navy blue, off-white, pink (or color of choice for skin), and brown worsted-weight yarn [4]

Size 1 (2.25 mm) double-pointed needles

Size D-3 (3.25 mm) crochet hook

Embroidery floss for eyes and mouth in the colors of your choice

Tapestry, embroidery, and sewing needles

Invisible or pink sewing thread

Yarn scraps or fiberfill for stuffing

Other: gold lace for crown, red ribbon for sash

BODY

Pants: Using navy blue yarn, CO 15 sts. Place sts onto 3 dpns and join.

Rnds 1–12: Knit.

Shirt: Cut navy blue yarn and tie on off-white.

Rnd 13: Knit.

Rnd 14: K2, M1, K3, M1, K6, M1, K4— 18 sts.

Rnds 15–19: Knit.

Place sts onto 2 needles and weave tog using Kitchener st (page 12).

Arms: Attach a 36"-long double strand of off-white at one side of body. Make st and then, using crochet hook, ch 9 sts. Turn and sl st into second ch and next 7 chs. Pull yarn through to other side and rep. If you want to add hands, pull a piece of pink yarn through end of arm with a crochet hook, make a knot, and fray ends a little for fingers.

HEAD

Using pink yarn, CO 11 sts. Place sts onto 3 dpns and join.

Rnds 1–10: Knit.

Gather and tie off at top, leaving 12" for nose and ears. Stuff lightly. Gather at bottom and leave 6" for attaching to body.

Nose and ears: Using yarn tail and tapestry needle, make French knots for nose and small, loose sts for ears.

Hair: With tapestry needle and brown yarn, make long sts all over head. See "Hairstyles" (page 62) for more ideas.

Eyes and mouth: With embroidery needle and floss, embroider eyes and mouth in any color you choose. Add eyebrows if you like.

(Continued on page 49)

FINISHING

Attach head to body: Pull yarn ends back and forth through head and body and then, using sewing needle and thread, attach head to body with small sts.

Crown: With a short length of gold lace make a round crown and st in place on head with sewing needle and thread.

Sash: Use a sewing needle and thread to st a piece of narrow ribbon from waist in front, over shoulder, and to waist in back for a royal sash.

Goldilocks and the Three Bears

SUPPLIES (For All Characters)

Gold, pink (or color of choice for skin), variegated, hot pink, brown, blue, baby blue, and green worsted-weight yarn (**4**)

Size 1 (2.25 mm) double-pointed needles

Sizes D-3 (3.25 mm) and C-2 (2.75 mm) crochet hooks

Embroidery floss for faces in black and the colors of your choice

Tapestry, embroidery, and sewing needles

Gold, brown, and invisible or pink sewing thread

Straight pins

Yarn scraps or fiberfill for stuffing

Other: beads for eyes, felt, lace, flowers or beads for trimming mother and father bears

GOLDILOCKS

Hair

Note: Start with the hair, because it will take some time to prepare.

Using gold yarn, CO 20 sts.

Using 2 needles, work back and forth in St st (knit RS rows, purl WS rows) for 20 rows. Tie off. Soak knit piece in water for a few minutes until piece is completely saturated. Let it sit until it is completely dry. When dry, unravel it and you will have the most incredible gold locks.

Body

Using variegated yarn, CO 14 sts. Place sts onto 3 dpns and join.

Rnds 1–10: Knit.

Rnd 11: K1, ssk, K1, K2tog, K2, K2tog, K1, ssk, K1—10 sts.

Rnds 12–19: Continue with original color or tie on hot pink yarn and knit.

Gather and tie off, leaving 6" for attaching to head.

Arms: Attach 36" of hot pink yarn at one side of body. Make st and then, using crochet hook, ch 8 sts. Turn and use smaller crochet hook to sl st in second ch from hook and rem 6 chs. Pull yarn through and rep on other side.

Head

Using pink yarn, CO 12 sts. Place sts onto 3 dpns and join.

Rnds 1–10: Knit.

Gather and tie off at top, leaving 12" for nose and ears. Stuff lightly. Gather at bottom and leave 6" for attaching to body.

Nose and ears: With yarn tail and tapestry needle, make little French knots on sides of head for ears and on front for nose.

Eyes and mouth: With embroidery needle and floss, add eyes and mouth.

Finishing

Tie off tail at bottom of body and hide it by pulling it up to head.

For a little extra interest, roll up bottom of hem so purl side shows.

Attach head to body: Pull yarn ends back and forth through head and body and then, using sewing needle and thread, attach head to body with small sts.

Hair: Unravel swatch of gold you knit. Cut pieces in lengths that suit you, approx 3" long. Lay them across top of head. Pin several pieces to middle of head and sew in place with sewing needle and matching thread. Rep, adding a few more pieces at a time, until Goldilocks has as many locks as you like.

Hair options: I've also made Goldilocks's hair by making very loose sts all over her head. But I like this more updated style.

BABY BEAR

Body

Using blue yarn, CO 13 sts for pants. Place sts onto 3 dpns and join.

Rnds 1–6: Knit.

Rnd 7: Purl.

Tie on brown yarn and knit 6 rnds.

Gather and tie off. Leave a 6" tail for attaching head to body.

Arms: Attach 36" of brown yarn to one side of body. Make st and then, using smaller crochet hook, ch 5 sts. Turn, sl st into second ch and into next 3 chs. Pull through and rep on other side. Hide yarn ends in head when you attach it.

Head

Using brown yarn, CO 12 sts, place sts onto 3 dpns, and join.

Rnd 1: Knit.

Rnd 2: K2, M1R, K1, M1L, knit to end of rnd—14 sts.

Rnds 3 and 5: Knit.

Rnd 4: K3, M1R, K1, M1L, knit to end of rnd—16 sts.

Rnd 6: K2, ssk, K1, K2tog, knit to end of rnd—14 sts.

Rnd 7: K1, ssk, K1, K2tog, knit to end of rnd—12 sts.

Rnd 8: Knit.

Weave top tog with Kitchener st (page 12). Leave approx 12" for crocheting ears.

Ears: Pull yarn through one corner of Kitchener st. With crochet hook, make loop and ch 4. Tie off, pull yarn back through and rep on other side.

Eyes and snout: With embroidery needle and floss, embroider black eyes and snout with small sts.

Finishing

Attach head to body: Stuff head lightly. Gather at bottom and leave 6" for attaching to body. Pull yarn ends back and forth through head and body and then, using sewing needle and thread, attach head to body with small sts.

Suspenders: Using single strand of yarn and C-2 (2.75 mm) crochet hook, ch 30 and tie off. With sewing needle and thread, sew suspenders to front waist, over shoulder, attach to back waist in middle, over other shoulder, and to front waist again.

MAMA BEAR

Mama Bear's dress is made by purling bottom and top and knitting a band in middle to give her a little shaping.

Body

Using baby blue yarn, CO 15 sts. Place sts onto 3 dpns and join.

Rnds 1–9: Purl.

Rnds 10–13: Knit.

Rnds 14–21: Purl.

Gather and tie off. Leave a 6" tail for attaching head to body.

Arms: Attach 36" of brown yarn at one side of body. Make st and then, using larger crochet hook, ch 7 sts. Turn and with smaller crochet hook, sl st into second ch and next 5 chs. Pull through to other side and rep.

Head

Using brown yarn, CO 14 sts. Place sts onto 3 dpns and join.

Rnds 1, 3, and 5: Knit.

Rnd 2: K3, M1R, K1, M1L, knit to end of rnd—16 sts.

Rnd 4: K4, M1R, K1, M1L, knit to end of rnd—18 sts.

Rnd 6: K3, ssk, K1, K2tog, knit to end of rnd—16 sts.

Rnd 7: K2, ssk, K1, K2tog, knit to end of rnd—14 sts.

Rnds 8–11: Knit.

Weave top tog using Kitchener st (page 12), leaving 24" tail for crocheting ears.

Ears: Pull yarn through at one end of Kitchener st and with crochet hook, ch 4. Pull yarn through to other side and rep. Hide yarn end inside head.

Eyes and snout: Use embroidery needle and black floss to st eyes and snout.

Finishing:

Attach head to body: Stuff head lightly. Gather at bottom and leave 6" for attaching to body. Pull yarn ends back and forth through head and body and then, using sewing needle and thread, attach head to body with small sts.

Accessories: Your Mama Bear may need to have earrings, pearls, a yarn bow in her hair, or a small lace shawl around her shoulders. Add all of these accessories using sewing needle and thread. Add a notion from a craft store or tie a bow with a piece of ribbon.

PAPA BEAR

Body

Using brown yarn, CO 17 sts. Place sts onto 3 dpns and join.

Rnds 1–8: Knit.

Cut brown yarn and tie on green yarn.

Rnd 9: Knit.

Rnd 10: Purl.

Rnds 11–17: Knit.

Gather and tie off. Leave 6" tail for attaching head to body.

Arms: Attach 36"-long double strand of green yarn at one side of body. Make st and then, holding strands tog and using crochet hook, ch 6 sts. Turn and sl st into second ch and next 4 chs. Pull through and rep on other side.

Head

Using brown yarn, CO 14 sts. Place sts onto 3 dpns and join.

Rnds 1, 2, 4, and 6: Knit.

Rnd 3: K3, M1R, K1, M1L, knit to end of rnd—16 sts.

Rnd 5: K4, M1R, K1, M1L, knit to end of rnd—18 sts.

Rnd 7: K3, ssk, K1, K2tog, knit to end of rnd—16 sts.

Rnd 8: K2, ssk, K1, K2tog, knit to end of rnd—14 sts.

Rnds 9–13: Knit.

Weave sts tog using Kitchener st (page 12), leaving 24" tail for crocheting ears.

Ears: Pull through yarn at corners of Kitchener st and, with crochet hook, ch 4 and attach tip of ear to side of head. Rep on other side.

Eyes and snout: Use embroidery needle and black floss to st eyes and snout.

Finishing

Attach head to body: Stuff head lightly. Gather at bottom and leave 6" for attaching to body. Pull yarn ends back and forth through head and body and then, using sewing needle and thread, attach head to body with small sts.

Tail: Attach brown yarn to center of back below green yarn and with smaller crochet hook, ch 4. Tie off tail at bottom and bring yarn up to middle of sweater in back to hide it.

Accessories: Papa Bear has a felt bow tie to dress him up. Cut it out using Snowman bow-tie pattern (page 23). St it on with sewing needle and thread.

Little Red Riding Hood, Grandma, and the Big Bad Wolf

Little Red Riding Hood is wearing the very special red cape that Grandma made for her. Grandma is all dressed up with her gold earrings. And if you want, you can give the Big Bad Wolf a little attitude by giving him a bow tie like the wolf with the Three Little Pigs!

SUPPLIES

Green, red, pink (or color of choice for skin), gold, white, and variegated or gray worsted-weight yarn 🔳4🔳

Size 1 (2.25 mm) double-pointed needles

Sizes D-3 (3.25 mm) and C-2 (2.25 mm) crochet hooks

Embroidery floss for eyes and mouths in the colors of your choice and gold metallic floss for Grandma's glasses

Tapestry, embroidery, and sewing needles

Invisible or pink sewing thread

Yarn scraps or fiberfill for stuffing

Other: gold beads for Grandma's earrings, black beads for the wolf's eyes, gray and red felt for the wolf's ears and bow tie (optional)

LITTLE RED RIDING HOOD
Body

Using red yarn, CO 15 sts. Place sts onto 3 dpns and join.

Rnds 1–15: Knit.

Gather and tie off at top, leaving 6" for attaching to head.

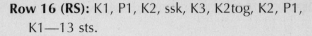

Arms: Attach 36" of red yarn at one side of body. Make st and then, using smaller crochet hook, ch 8. Change to larger hook. Turn and sl st into 2nd st and next 6 chs. Pull yarn through and rep on other side.

Head

Using pink, CO 10 sts. Place sts onto 3 dpns and join.

Rnds 1–9: Knit.

Gather and tie off at top, leaving 12" tail for nose and ears. Stuff lightly and gather at bottom, leaving 6" for attaching to body.

Nose and ears: Using yarn tail and tapestry needle, make small French knots on each side of head for ears and one on front for nose.

Eyes and mouth: With embroidery needle and floss, make small French knots for eyes and st a smiling mouth.

Attach head to body: Pull yarn ends back and forth through head and body and then, using sewing needle and thread, attach head to body with small sts.

Hair: With tapestry needle and gold yarn, make small loose sts all over head.

Hooded Cape

Using red yarn, CO 15 sts onto 1 dpn. Cape is worked back and forth on 2 needles.

Rows 1–3: K1, *P1, K1, rep from * to end.

Row 4 and all even-numbered rows (RS): K1, P1, K11, P1, K1.

Row 5 and all odd-numbered rows (WS): K1, P13, K1.

Continue until there are 15 rows, ending with WS row as follows:

Row 15: K1, P1, K2, ssk, K3, K2tog, K2, P1, K1—13 sts.

Row 16 (RS): K1, P1, K2, ssk, K3, K2tog, K2, P1, K1—13 sts.

Row 17: K1, P11, K1.

Row 18: K1, P1, K2, ssk, K1, K2tog, K2, P1, K1—11 sts.

Row 19 and all odd-numbered rows: (WS) K1, P9, K1.

Row 20 and all even-numbered rows: (RS) K1, P1, K7, P1, K1.

Continue until you've worked 26 rows in total, ending with RS row.

Next row: K1, P4, P2tog, P3, K1—10 sts.

Put the 10 st on 2 needles. Hold needles parallel and weave sts tog with Kitchener st (page 12). Tie a knot in last st and hide yarn ends inside hood.

Cape tie: Thread tapestry needle with approx 8" of red yarn and take small sts at point of last decrease to attach yarn and tie a bow.

GRANDMA
Body

Using green yarn, CO 17 sts. Place sts onto 3 dpns and join.

Rnd 1: Knit.

Rnds 2–5: K1, *P1, K1, rep from * to end of rnd.

Rnds 6–15: Knit.

Gather and tie off at top, leaving 6" for attaching to head.

Arms: Attach 36" of green yarn at one side of body. Make st and then, using smaller crochet hook, ch 10 sts. Change to larger hook. Turn and sl st into 2nd ch and next 8 chs. Pull through and rep on other side.

Head

Using pink yarn, CO 16 sts. Place sts onto 3 dpns and join.

Rnds 1–12: Knit.

Gather and tie off at top, leaving 12" tail for nose and ears. Stuff lightly and gather at bottom, leaving 6" for attaching to body.

Ears and nose: With tapestry needle and yarn tail, make French knots on either side of head for ears and one large French knot in middle of face for nose. With sewing needle and thread, tack on small beads for earrings.

Mouth and eyes: With embroidery needle and floss, use the colors of your choice to embroider mouth and make small knots for eyes. To add glasses made with gold metallic embroidery floss, take a st from one ear to one eye. Make a little circle with thread and tack in place. Then make a small st over nose, make another circle, tack in place, and make another small st to other ear.

Hair: Using white yarn and tapestry needle, make long sts from front and back of head to top. Then in the middle of those threads add large, loose sts (curls) for a nice little bun.

Attach head to body: Pull yarn ends back and forth through head and body and then, using sewing needle and thread, attach head to body with small sts.

THE BIG BAD WOLF

In nature there are gray, brownish gray, and black wolves; I've made wolf puppets in all those colors. I like the variegated wolf best, but his wicked teeth aren't as obvious as they are on the gray wolf.

Body

Using gray or variegated yarn, CO 18 sts. Place sts onto 3 dpns and join.

Rnds 1–18: Knit.

Gather and tie off. Leave 6" tail for attaching head to body.

Legs and paws: Attach 2 strands of yarn, 36" long, at one side of body. Make st and then, holding strands tog and using larger crochet hook, ch 6 sts. Turn and sl st into second ch and next 4 chs. Pull through to other side and rep.

Head

Using gray or variegated yarn, CO 16 sts. Place sts onto 3 dpns and join.

Rnds 1, 3, 5, and 7: Knit.

Rnd 2: K4, M1R, K1, M1L, knit to end—18 sts.

Rnd 4: K5, M1R, K1, M1L, knit to end—20 sts.

Rnd 6: K6, M1R, K1, M1L, knit to end—22 sts.

Rnd 8: K5, ssk, K1, K2tog, knit to end—20 sts.

Rnd 9: K4, ssk, K1, K2tog, knit to end—18 sts.

Rnd 10: K3, ssk, K1, K2tog, knit to end—16 sts.

Rnd 11: K2, ssk, K1, K2tog, knit to end—14 sts.

Put 14 sts on 2 needles and weave tog with Kitchener st (page 12), leaving 36" tail for ears.

Ears: Using crochet hook, draw tail through edges of head. Ch 5 and pull back through head. Rep on other side. Tie off yarn. If desired, sew on small, pointed felt ears.

Finishing

Attach head to body: Stuff head lightly and gather at bottom, leaving 6" for attaching to body. Pull yarn ends back and forth through head and body and then, using sewing needle and thread, attach head to body with small sts.

Tail: With yarn tail at beg of body, make a st and ch 4 with crochet hook. Tie off and fray ends.

Snout and eyes: Using embroidery needle, make a few sts with black floss on snout and a slash of black for mouth. Make 2 vertical sts with white floss for fangs across mouth. With sewing needle and thread, sew on black beads for eye.

Tie (optional): Cut a tie out of felt using Snowman bow-tie pattern (page 23) and st on under chin, or tie a ribbon around wolf's neck.

Three Little Pigs

SUPPLIES

Pink (or color of choice for skin), blue, yellow, and variegated worsted-weight yarn **4**

Size 1 (2.25 mm) double-pointed needles

Sizes D-3 (3.25 mm) and C-2 (2.75 mm) crochet hooks

Black embroidery floss for noses

Tapestry, embroidery, and sewing needles

Invisible or pink sewing thread

Yarn scraps or fiberfill for stuffing

Straight pins

Other: black beads for eyes

THE BASIC BODIES

Each Little Pig should have its own look. Use different colors of yarn or add a seed stitch to the bottom or top of one body. Add suspenders for one of them and a vest or tie for the other two.

You can do the ears with little pieces of felt, and rather than crocheting a little circle for the snout, you can just use a few strands of embroidery floss.

Body 1

Using variegated yarn, CO 16 sts. Place sts onto 3 dpns and join.

Rnds 1–15: Knit.

Gather and tie off. Leave a 6" tail for attaching head to body.

Bodies 2 and 3

Using blue or yellow yarn, CO 16 sts. Place sts onto 3 dpns and join.

Rnds 1–7: Knit.

Rnd 8: Purl.

Cut yarn and tie on pink yarn.

Rnds 9–15: Knit.

Gather and tie off. Leave a 6" tail for attaching head to body.

Suspenders: With smaller crochet hook, ch 18–24 sts, leaving a little length at each end for attaching to body at the purl row in front, at center of back, and again in front. Attach suspenders by pulling yarn through on one side in front. St in place. Then draw ch up over shoulder, secure it in middle of back with a sewing needle and thread, draw it up over other shoulder, and tack in place on other side in front. Secure with needle and thread.

ARMS

Attach 36" of pink yarn at one shoulder. Make st and then, using larger crochet hook, ch 7 sts. Using the smaller crochet hook, turn and sl st into second ch and next 5 chs. Pull through and rep on other side.

HEAD

Using pink yarn, CO 14 sts. Place sts onto 3 dpns and join.

Rnds 1, 3, 5, and 7: Knit.

Rnd 2: K3, M1R, K1, M1L, knit to end of rnd—16 sts.

Rnd 4: K4, M1R, K1, M1L, knit to end of rnd—18 sts.

Rnd 6: K5, M1R, K1, M1L, knit to end of rnd—20 sts.

Rnd 8: K4, ssk, K1, K2tog, knit to end of rnd—18 sts.

Rnd 9: K3, ssk, K1, K2tog, knit to end of rnd—16 sts.

Rnd 10: K2, ssk, K1, K2tog, knit to end of rnd—14 sts.

Rnd 11: Knit.

Place the 14 sts on 2 dpns and weave tog using Kitchener st (page 12), leaving 48" tail for crocheting ears.

Ears: Pull yarn tail back through top of Kitchener st to begin working ear on left side of head. This helps to pull top of head tog for a more piglike shape. With crochet hook, ch 4 sts. Pull through and rep on other side.

Snout: Mark middle of face with pin. Attach pink yarn a half st to right of pin. With smaller crochet hook, ch 6. Attach on other side of pin and anchor in place at top with pink thread. Embroider 2 black sts inside snout.

Eyes: Add tiny black or pink beads close to center of head.

Finishing

Attach head to body: Stuff head lightly with leftover yarn. Gather bottom, leaving 6" tail for attaching head to body. Pull yarn end from head through body and back again. Do the same with yarn end from body to hide these ends. Then, using a sewing needle and thread, st head to body with invisible sts to give more stability.

Tail (optional): Attach 12" of pink yarn toward bottom of center back. With smaller crochet hook, ch 4 and sew into circle.

CREATING YOUR OWN CHARACTERS

After you've made a few of the puppets following the patterns in this book, you'll begin to see ideas for special puppets everywhere. A bride and groom, a new baby, a soccer player, or a favorite pet are all great reasons to make very personal puppets. My grandsons often come to me with ideas for a character. "Grandma, can you make this puppet?" Then the fun begins. What is the right shape for the head and the body? What are the right colors? Will we need any special accessories like masks or capes? Then it's up to me to make the puppet come to life.

This section gives you some of the components for creating the puppets in your imagination. There are seven basic shapes for the heads: round, oval, pear-shaped, squared off, flattop, teardrop, and elliptical. Add to these four different basic body shapes, plus the knit and purl variations, and the number of combinations is endless.

Over the years I've experimented with many hairstyles. Goldilocks's untamed gold ringlets and the wizard's flowing beard are two of my favorites. I've recently discovered how to do spikes for a couple of little boy puppets, and I like the look of the balding Santa and the clowns.

This yellow-haired puppet is a recent creation based on a drawing by my grandson Max. Max chose all the yarn and deemed the final product "perfect."

BODY SHAPES

Basic Adult

CO 15 sts. Place sts onto 3 dpns and join. Knit 15 rnds. Gather at top and tie off.

Basic Child

CO 12 sts. Place sts onto 3 dpns and join. Knit 12 rnds. Gather at top and tie off.

Knit and Purl Variations

While most puppets are done in the round so you knit every st, purling some sts can create a different look.

Ribbing

CO 14 sts. Place sts onto 3 dpns and join.

Rnds 1–14: (K1, P1) around.

Gather at top and tie off.

Seed Stitch

CO 14 sts. Place sts onto 3 dpns and join.

Rnd 1: (K1, P1) around.

Rnd 2: (P1, K1) around.

Rep rnds 1 and 2 until body is desired height. Gather at top and tie off.

Muscleman

CO 14 sts. Place sts onto 3 dpns and join.

Rnds 1–10, 16, and 18–21: Knit.

Rnd 11: Tie on contrasting color yarn and knit.

Rnds 12–14: Knit.

Rnd 15: (K3, M1R, K1, M1L, K3) twice— 18 sts.

Rnd 17: (K3, M1R, K3, M1L, K3) twice—22 sts.

Divide sts onto 2 dpns and hold needles parallel. Weave sts tog using Kitchener st (page 12). When you have just 1 st left, tie off and then thread yarn back through to beg. This will give shoulders more of a rounded look.

Princess

This shaping will give you a full skirt, a small waist, and broad shoulders.

CO 22 sts. Place sts onto 3 dpns and join.

Rnds 1 and 2: Purl.

Rnds 3–5, 7, 9, 11, 13–15, and 17–19: Knit.

Rnd 6: K1, ssk, K7, K2tog, K10—20 sts.

Rnd 8: K1, ssk, K5, K2tog, K10—18 sts.

Rnd 10: K1, ssk, K3, K2tog, K10—16 sts.

Rnd 12: K1, ssk, K1, K2tog, K2, ssk, K3, K2tog, K1—12 sts.

Rnd 16: K2, M1R, K1, M1L, K9—14 sts.

Put the rem sts on 2 needles and weave sts tog using Kitchener st (page 12). When you have just 1 st left, tie off and then thread yarn back through to beg. This will give shoulders more of a rounded look.

Robes

Start with 24–30 sts and then evenly decrease until you have length and width you need. The wizard pattern calls for equal decreases in back and front so there is one front slant and one back slant.

CO 28 sts. Place sts onto 3 dpns and join.

Rnd 1: Purl.

Rnds 2 and 3: Knit.

Rnd 4: K12, K2tog, K12, K2tog—26 sts.

Cont working 2 rnds even, then dec on every 3rd rnd as foll:

Rnd 7: K11, K2tog, K11, K2tog—24 sts.

Rnd 10: K10, K2tog, K10, K2tog—22 sts.

Rnd 13: K9, K2tog, K9, K2tog—20 sts.

Rnd 16: K8, K2tog, K8, K2tog—18 sts.

Rnd 19: K7, K2tog, K7, K2tog—16 sts.

Rnd 22: K6, K2tog, K6, K2tog—14 sts.

Rnd 25: K5, K2tog, K5, K2tog—12 sts.

Rnd 26: Knit.

Gather and tie off. Leave 6" tail for attaching body to head.

ARMS

There are as many variations for arms as there are for heads and bodies. Wolves and bears have short, thick, two-strand arms and paws. The monkeys have long, slender arms. I sometimes think I know just what will work best for arm length and thickness, but when I finish it just doesn't work for that little personality. I like to crochet the arms on my finger puppets. If you don't crochet, you can use a three-stitch I-cord knit to the desired length for the arms on your puppets. Here are the basic crochet instructions, and there are also guidelines in each pattern. But for those you create on your own you will get to experiment.

Use a tapestry needle to join a single strand of yarn from the inside of the puppet at one shoulder. Take one stitch and then, using a size D-3 (3.25 mm) crochet hook, chain 8. Turn and single crochet in the second chain from the hook and in each of the remaining six chains. Pull the yarn through the body to the other side and repeat. Pull the yarn into the body and secure it by drawing it up through the head or tying a knot inside the body.

Sometimes for variety or because the yarn is harder to work with, I use a smaller crochet hook after the turn. A size C-2 (2.75 mm) hook works well for this. Keep one on hand.

Occasionally it seems necessary to add hands to the puppets. All it takes is inserting a crochet hook into the end of the arm and pulling through a short loop of yarn. Then pull the yarn ends back through the loop and pull tight; cut off any excess. If you fray the ends a little it will look like fingers.

| Round | Oval | Pear-shaped | Teardrop | Flattop | Squared off | Elliptical |

HEADS

There are as many variations in puppet heads as there are in human, animal, and cartoon heads. There are seven basic shapes suggested here but you can vary that by adding rounds or stitches, or increasing or decreasing to add extra shaping.

Round

Adult: CO 14 sts. Place sts onto 3 dpns and join. Knit 11 rnds.

Child: CO 10 sts. Place sts onto 3 dpns and join. Knit 8 rnds.

Gather top, stuff lightly with extra yarn or fiberfill, and gather at bottom.

Oval

CO 11 sts. Place sts onto 3 dpns and join. Knit 14 rnds.

Gather top, stuff lightly with extra yarn or fiberfill, and gather at bottom.

Pear-Shaped

CO 11 sts. Place sts onto 3 dpns and join. Knit 13 rnds.

Gather top, stuff lightly with extra yarn or fiberfill, and gather at bottom.

Before adding nose and ears, with matching-colored thread, run a gathering st through middle of oval and pull thread to create pear shape. The thread should be invisible if you catch the back of each st.

Teardrop

CO 16 sts. Place sts onto 3 dpns and join.

Rnds 1–6, 8, and 10 : Knit.

Rnd 7: (Ssk, K4, K2tog) twice—12 sts.

Rnd 9: (Ssk, K2, K2tog) twice—8 sts.

Rnd 11: (Ssk, K2tog) twice—4 sts.

Gather top, stuff lightly with extra yarn or fiberfill, and gather at bottom.

Flattop

Follow the directions for round but instead of gathering the top, put the 14 sts on 2 needles and weave sts tog using Kitchener st (page 12). This head is good for characters with ears at the top of their heads, such as kittens and dogs.

Squared Off

CO 10 sts. Place sts onto 3 dpns and join.

Rnds 1 and 2, 4, 6–8, 10, and 12: Knit.

Rnd 3: (K2, M1R, K1, M1L, K2) twice—14 sts.

Rnd 5: (K2, M1R, K3, M1L, K2) twice—18 sts.

Rnd 9: (K1, ssk, K3, K2tog, K1) twice—14 sts.

Rnd 11: (K1, ssk, K1, K2tog, K1) twice—10 sts.

Gather top or weave tog using Kitchener st (page 12). Stuff lightly with extra yarn or fiberfill and gather bottom.

Elliptical

This shape is wonderful for cartoon characters.

CO 10 sts. Place sts onto 3 dpns and join.

Rnds 1 and 2, 4, 6 and 7, 9, and 11: Knit.

Rnd 3: (K1, M1R, K3, M1L, K1) twice—14 sts.

Rnd 5: (K1, M1R, K5, M1L, K1) twice—18 sts.

Rnd 8: (K1, ssk, K3, K2tog, K1) twice—14 sts.

Rnd 10: (K1, ssk, K1, K2tog, K1) twice—10 sts.

Gather top, stuff lightly with extra yarn or fiberfill, and gather at bottom.

Each of these head shapes can be varied by adding or subtracting a rnd or st. If you need a large adult figure you may want to cast on 18 sts and knit 16 rnds. A very small child or teddy bear character may only need 10 sts and 11 rnds.

ANIMAL HEADS

Some animal heads are completely different in shape from human heads. I struggled with animal heads until I opened a stocking pattern book and found a pattern for a Christmas stocking tree ornament. When I looked at that tiny stocking suddenly I could see that the foot would be a perfect puppet face for giraffes, elephants, reindeers, and others. Now I use an adaptation of a stocking gusset. See directions for Reindeer (page 24) and Giraffe (page 37) for examples. Be sure to keep the yarn-over stitches fairly tight so there are no gaps at the sides of the heads.

EARS

For most of the human characters, just a little stitch on each side of the head will be enough to make ears. With a pin, mark the placement on each side of the head. Bring the yarn from the inside of the head and make a vertical stitch. Often I add another stitch around the top of that stitch. That is called a whip-stitch when you make a number of loops, and for extra-large ears you may want to do more than one.

For animals there are two methods. One is to crochet three or four chains, tie off, pull back through head, and repeat on the other side. Another is to cut ears out of felt and stitch them in place with tiny stitches. For the reindeer I used felt. For the bear family, chaining seemed a better solution.

NOSES

The easiest way to create a small nose is to bring a single strand of yarn from the inside of the head. Make a small French knot and pull the yarn back through a half stitch away from where you brought the yarn through. For a witch or wizard or a larger puppet use double strands of yarn. Experiment with nose stitches. Sometimes I make a horizontal stitch across two stitches and then make a vertical knot over that. Each nose is unique.

Embroidery Stitches

Most of the embroidery used to embellish these puppets is made of simple straight stitches.

Ears and noses are usually made with French knots, which are slightly more complicated. Wrap the yarn or floss around the needle and secure to the puppet.

French knot

MOUTHS AND EYES

Use a variety of embroidery floss to make the mouths and eyes. Make a V for a smiling mouth and a straight line for a more serious puppet.

For the eyes, make a small French knot using two or three strands of floss. Add a straight line over that if you like the look. Some characters need eyebrows or lines to indicate eyelashes. This is where you can really see the personality of the puppet come alive.

Glasses

See Little Red Riding Hood's grandma (page 53).

HAIRSTYLES

Basic Hair

The most basic hairstyle requires just a tapestry needle and a single strand of yarn stitched back and forth over the head. I usually start on the left or right side where a part might be, and then take long stitches from there to the sides and back.

Chignons

Make long stitches from the front, back, and sides to a point on the top of the head. When you have covered all the head, make some very loose stitches on the top for curls.

Spikes

Sew on short lengths of yarn. When the yarn is almost used up, pull the end up and just leave it sticking up.

Long Hair

Cut 10 or more pieces of yarn twice the length you want for the hair. Lay them parallel on a flat surface and run a matching thread through the middle of them. Then pin the middle of the yarn to the middle of the head and tack in place. For the witch, you can let the hair fly. For some other puppets, you may want to tack the strands down at the sides.

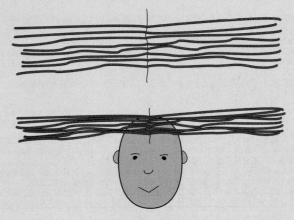

Braids

Follow the directions for long hair including the stitches on the sides of the head. Divide the hair into six equal parts—three on each side of the head—and braid them. Tie them together close to the bottom with narrow ribbons or short lengths of yarn.

Curly Locks

There are two way to make curls. The easiest is to sew loose stitches all over the head in a fairly random manner so it doesn't look like ringlets.

The second method is the Goldilocks look. Using two double-pointed needles, cast on 20 stitches and knit 20 rows. Soak the piece in water and leave it to dry. Unravel it carefully and cut it into somewhat even lengths. Stitch the middle of each length to the middle of the head and don't bother to stitch down the sides. It's a wild and crazy look.

Beards and Mustaches

For a short, curly beard, use the first method given for curly hair. Make small stitches in a random manner all over the chin and under the nose.

For the long wizard beard, cut lengths of yarn twice the length you want for the beard. Lay the pieces parallel on a flat surface and run a matching thread through the middle of them. Fold the lengths in half and pin to the chin. Stitch in place and take two small stitches with the yarn for a mustache.

ACCESSORIES

Look around your house with an eye for puppets and you will be amazed at how much you have for dressing up your little characters. Old jewelry, leftover lace, and pieces of felt all make fabulous accessories.

Felt is easily stretched into hat shapes that are perfect for finger puppets. Start with a basic half circle. Wrap it into a cone. Stitch it together on the overlap and leave it. Or you may want to stretch out the bottom to create a brim.

Many craft stores have miniature hats in many colors, styles, and materials. You can also find beads in the jewelry section.

It's a lot of fun to create a personalized puppet for someone special. The punk rock character shown above right is one my son and I worked on together in the early 1980s. The green-eyed puppet came from the imagination of my grandson Will, 25 years later.

ABOUT THE AUTHOR

Meg Leach comes from a family of teachers—her grandmother, mother, aunts, uncles, and sisters. Her own teaching career has included teaching pre-schoolers how to play together, teaching high school seniors about child development, teaching university students about family systems, and most recently teaching business executives organization development practices.

For many years she knit the usual scarves, sweaters, mittens, and Christmas stockings. But nothing has been as much fun or as creative to knit as the finger puppets she learned to make 40 years ago. Grandchildren have turned that fun into a grand passion. They can always think of new characters to create together.

This book is her way of combining the joy of teaching others with the joy of knitting finger puppets.